The Digest Enthusiast

Book One   **January 2015**

D1810367

Editor Arkay Olgar
Contributing Editor D. Blake Werts
Design Ida August

Cover by Joe Wehrle, Jr.
Cartoons by Bob Vojtko

Thanks to Joyce Erland, Ann Jansen, Tim Joy, Elizabeth McPhee, Janice Newton, Dee Dee Ploog, Midge Raymond and Robert Snashall.

Visit us online at LarquePress.com/DigestEnthusiast for current and vintage digest covers and news. Join our privacy-secure mailing list, used exclusively for updates on The Digest Enthusiast and Larque Press, at LarquePress.com.

Editor's Notes

"The Executioner's Signature" by George Fielding Eliot is the lead story, billed as a "new novel" on the cover of *The Saint Detective Magazine*, May 1957. Read it the summer of 2014, 57 years after its debut. A terrific story in a classic digest magazine. How many copies of this issue still exist? How often are they reread or discovered for the first time nearly six decades later? No way to know, but there's no doubt these old digests will continue to be discovered and read for years to come. It's one of the intrinsic advantages of print.

Don't get me wrong, I have nothing against digital media. Plans for this effort include publishing in multiple formats. Yet I can't help wonder if today's ebooks will even be readable on tablets 57 years from now? Who can imagine finding a collection of ebooks to browse through at flea markets or estate sales, or to bid for on eBay? Maybe it's simply a new capability coming from the cloud.

Closer to home, let's get back to digests. D. Blake Werts (*Copy This!*), Rob Imes (*Ditkomania*) and I were chatting across email. Pulp magazines had—and have—their champions, but we couldn't recall one for their stepchild. It seemed like time enough. *The Digest Collector*, Rob's suggested title, became

The Digest Enthusiast (*TDE*), coined by Blake. A name to encompass readers and collectors. And since our focus is primarily on digests of genre fiction, it seems appropriate to include content about digests as well as a few original works of fiction. On that front, we're pleased to present "A Darker Night" from the multi-talented Joe Wehrle, Jr., who also provided its splash page illustration. The fanciful painting on our debut cover is also Joe's work, created as a tribute to Ed Emshwiller.

Two crime stories come from Lesann Berry and from Richard Krauss, whose piece is illustrated by Michael Neno.

Rob Imes provides a rousing defense of digests, along with a little of their origins. And Rob hooked us up with Larry Johnson (*Tales of Fantasy*) who pays tribute to H.L. Gold's run as editor of *Galaxy Science Fiction*. Our resident "Bad Mags" expert, Tom Brinkmann, exposes us to the girlie digests of Myron Fass. A cadre of enthusiastic contributors provides the scoop on *The Big Story*, and reviews of select issues of *Fate* magazine, Gary Lovisi's *Paperback Parade*, and *Coronet*. Bob Vojtko brightens every page on which his gag cartoons appear.

Our interviews this time out

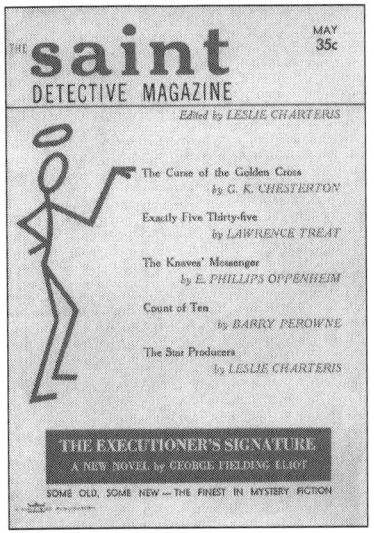

Asimov's 28,348
Ellery Queen 28,749
Fate magazine 13,000
   (estimate) 2013 & 2014[1]
Fantasy & Science Fiction 26,000[2]
Fantasy & Science Fiction 33,500
   2013 & 2014[1]
Granta 34,200
   (US 14,200, UK 20,000)
Paris Review ~6,000 subscribers[3]
Reader's Digest 4,288,529 2013[1]
Reader's Digest 3,000,000
Tin House >12,000

Send the Average Total Paid Circulation, along with the title, date and year of publication, to arkay@larquepress.com or

Larque Press
6327 SW Capitol Hwy,
Suite C #293
Portland, OR 97239

include Gordon Van Gelder (*Fantasy and Science Fiction* editor and publisher), Phyllis Galde (*Fate* magazine editor-in-chief) and avid Archie digest collector Matthew Turcotte.

Now here's a request. We're anxious to collect historical data on the circulation of digests based on the publisher's annual Statements of Ownership, Management and Circulation. These reports include several numbers. To keep things simple let's focus on the Total Paid Circulation for the average number of copies over the preceding twelve months. Other sources of paid circulation are also welcome.

What follows are circulation numbers for some of today's digests. The numbers are based on the circulation listed on their advertising rate cards, pulled from their websites in early December 2014, and other sources as noted.

Alfred Hitchcock 21,207
Alfred Hitchcock 48,424
   (estimate) 2014[1]
Analog 33,642

We'll track the data on our website at LarquePress.com.

Special thanks to contributing editor, D. Blake Werts, for a multitude of assistance on this first edition. It wouldn't be the same without you, Blake!

And thank you, dear reader, for your interest in the world of digests. We'd love to hear from you—what you think of our debut and what you'd like to see in future editions. Please join us on the forum at LarquePress.com or write me directly at arkay@larquepress.com

Until next time,
-Arkay Olgar

[1] Gale Directory Library
[2] Average paid circulation 12 months ending Sept. 30, 2005
[3] New York Times Feb. 6, 2005 "Does The Paris Review Get a Second Act?"

Phyllis Galde
Interview with Fate magazine's
editor and publisher.

In the late 1940's, Raymond A. Palmer was editor of *Amazing Stories* and Curtis Fuller was editor of *Flying*, both published by Ziff-Davis. When the company announced they'd move their offices from Chicago to New York as of 1950, it sparked a new publishing venture.

As early as 1947, Palmer was moonlighting three blocks away from Ziff-Davis, on Clark Street, home of the newly minted Clark Publishing company, where *Fate* was cast. The publication debuted as a quarterly digest-sized magazine in the spring of 1948 capitalizing on the fervor of Kenneth Arnold's famous sighting of nine unidentified flying objects while flying near Mt. Rainier in Washington State on June 24, 1947. Palmer and Curtis knew that stories of unexplained phenomenon like UFOs were widely popular with readers and decided the market would support a magazine completely dedicated to other-worldly subjects.

In the early days *Fate* was mostly under Palmer's direction. He single-handedly wrote much of the early issues under various pseudonyms, including that of the editor, Robert

N. Webster. Curtis Fuller kept busy editing *Flying* and being prime caregiver to his children while his wife Mary battled tuberculosis in a TB sanitarium. Fuller's main contribution was his "I See By the Papers" column, which began in 1952.

Both Mary and Curt Fuller had journalistic backgrounds, with less sensational leanings than Palmer. When Mary's health improved the Fullers took a larger role in the magazine and worked to ensure that however outlandish a story seemed, it was factually grounded. For example, they didn't allow a second controversial Shaver Mystery story to appear after the first.

Not long after Palmer moved from Chicago to Amherst, Wisconsin, the Fullers bought out his interest in the magazine, and Mary Fuller took over as editor. In 1953 Palmer went on to launch *Mystic Magazine*, a fiction digest intended to appeal to much the same audience as *Fate*.

Under the Fullers' direction *Fate* grew in popularity and by the mid-1970s had a reported circulation of about 200K.

Jerome Clark, a noted UFO historian and researcher, served

DONALD KEYHOE—HOW THE SAUCERS FLY

November 1954 35¢

FATE
AND
M A G A Z I N E

BOAC's
FLYING
JELLYFISH

AIR CHIEF MARSHAL
LORD DOWDING
" WHY I BELIEVE
IN SAUCERS "

Fate #56, Volume 7, #11 Nov. 1954 with editor Robert N. Webster, executive editor Mary Fuller and editorial consultant Curtis Fuller.

as editor from 1976 to 1989. But interest in *Fate* was declining and eventually the Fullers were looking to sell the magazine.

Earlier, Hugh Heffner reportedly had an interest in doing a slick, pop science magazine to compete with Bob Guccione's *Omni*, but with paranormal content. Unfortunately, by the time the Fullers were ready to sell, Heffner was no longer interested. That left them with few options. Reluctantly, they sold *Fate* to Llewellyn Publications

Fate #497, Volume 44, #8 Aug. 1991 with Curtis Fuller (1912–1991) tribute.

in 1988, reportedly for not much.

Owned by Carl Weschcke, Llewellyn Publications' focus was on the occult, which worried the Fullers about the future direction of the magazine. The Fullers' position was, as Mary put it, "We don't have to believe it ourselves, but it has to be capable of belief." Nevertheless, Llewellyn purchased the magazine in 1988.

Three years earlier, Phyllis Galde had been hired as a book editor at Llewellyn. When Weschcke bought *Fate*, he assigned Donald Michael Kraig as the new editor and Galde managed to land a job helping him. Kraig and Galde tried to keep *Fate* "pure," while Weschcke reportedly wanted it to be an advertorial for Llewellyn books.

Sales of *Fate* continued a slow decline. By 1994, in a move to increase its appeal to potential advertisers, *Fate* grew to full magazine size and was printed in full color on glossy stock. Unfortunately, even that didn't turn things around.

Eventually, Weschcke was ready to end the magazine. Reportedly, his wife Sandra, encouraged him to sell instead. In 1999, Sandra called David Godwin and asked if the he and his partner, Phyllis Galde, would help out while Llewellyn was in the process of trying to sell it. Galde immediately saw how much money was being wasted at the magazine. She and Godwin ran things for two years, cutting costs drastically. But Llewellyn still wanted to sell, so Galde, with the help of her bank, bought it.

Galde recalled walking out of the building after the sale was complete, feeling the presence of Curt and Mary Fuller, who had both passed on, scolding her to do a good job, having not been happy with the influence Weschcke had made.

Galde still runs *Fate*, and Galde Press, from her modest office in Lakeville, Minnesota. *The Digest Enthusiast* interviewed Galde via phone in late September, 2014.

The Digest Enthusiast: The job of editor of *Fate* magazine must have been a dream come true. Tell us about the journey that brought you there.

Phyllis Galde: I was an editor at Llewellyn Publications in Saint Paul. I started there in about 1985. Previously to that I taught school,

References for introduction:
Phyllis Galde
The Man From Mars by Fred Nadis
noufors.com/Jerome_Clark.htm
The Paracast March 23, 2014

and then one day I just decided to quit. A couple of years later after I had kind of a retreat at our old haunted farm house in North Dakota, I was in Minneapolis with my dad and I just decided to call Llewellyn. It's funny my hand just opened up the phone book and my finger went on "Llewellyn." It's just like something took over me and inspired me to do that. I applied for a job there as an editor and I got it.

In 1988, Llewellyn decided to purchase *Fate* magazine from Curtis and Mary Fuller in Chicago. So they transferred the whole business, hired a truck and brought everything up here. Don Kraig was the editor in chief. I was working as a book editor and I said "Me, me, me! Hire me for managing editor." And finally he got permission to hire me. He and I worked on the magazine for several years and eventually he quit and went off to California. So then luckily, I sort of fell into being the editor in chief. We had a small staff at Llewellyn that worked part time on books and part time on the magazine.

My mother had died a few years previously, and my dad had come to stay with me. I was driving down the street in Apple Valley, a small suburb near where I live, and I heard a voice in my head, "Spend this time with your dad." So I did. I handed in my resignation to Llewellyn. They were mortified, they didn't want me to quit, but I had three months with my dad and then he had a severe stroke. So I'm so glad I listened to that voice. We had some good times. We visited some relatives and the following year he died.

My life partner, David Godwin and I were working with books,

Fate #19, Volume 4, #3 Apr. 1951 with editor Robert N. Webster and managing editor Beatrice Mahaffey.

in my book publishing business, this was 2001 I guess, when Sandra Weschcke, the owner's wife called and asked me to come back and help with *Fate*. They had decided to sell it or kill it, cease publication, whatever, so David and I went in there, and I told Sandra she could get rid of everybody else. David and I could do this. So we saved them a couple of hundred thousand dollars a year because they had an unnecessary staff and of course they still wanted to sell it and again I happened to be in the right place at the right time. Having had experience on it, and Carl [Weschcke] was very fond of *Fate*. He didn't want it to totally cease publication so he sold it to me and the bank.

So it was really a labor of love for David and I. We enjoyed working on it. It was certainly not a money making business, which is why Llewellyn chose to get rid of it. It was costing more than it was making, and for

Fate #32, Volume 5, #8 Nov. 1952 with editor Robert N. Webster.

David and I too, we worked and lived very frugally. It was a home-based business so we were able to keep it going. And then David died, it will be three years ago in October.

It was a very difficult, challenging time for me. I was working all alone. We had a few interns here and there, but it was a real challenge. This includes our publishing company. Fortunately, we had everything set up on computer and we had all the same programs that Llewellyn had saved all the archive material for *Fate* in.

Many of the books that we have published are metaphysical, paranormal, so the subject matter fits in with *Fate* very well. And Galde Press kind of subsidized, helped pay for *Fate*. Back in the day book publishing was much more lucrative than magazine publishing. It helped pay the bills.

TDE: What is it about publishing that appeals to you?

PG: I was a school teacher for twelve years and I guess I'm still correcting papers. Now it's articles. You know being an English teacher, this is just a continuation. I've always been interested in the paranormal. I grew up in a haunted house in North Dakota and my earliest memories as a small child were seeing a ghost in the doorway of my bedroom.

Then, when I was about twenty-five, I was home visiting mom and dad they told me my grandfather had died in that room. Oh, if they would've told me that I wouldn't have been so scared when I was a little kid. Because I saw this image every night standing in the doorway. And really, I'm sure he was there as more of a guardian angel protecting and watching over his family.

TDE: Have you had other paranormal experiences?

PG: Oh yes, oh yes, that would be a whole 'nother interview. I've had many, many paranormal experiences, with human and non-human entities, through the years. It used to scare the crap out of me, but I'm much more comfortable with it now.

When I was little, seeing my grandfather's ghost was like aaaagggghhhhh! But I didn't know who it was. I thought it was a bad thing, here to do something bad. So I was terrified.

But now it's different. Certainly repetition is part of it, and increased understanding of life after death. I mean that's really the whole crux of *Fate*. Why it's survived so long. Proof of survival and true life experiences. When you've read thousands of stories that are similar it gets to be less scary. I don't know if it's a blessing or a curse but I seem to see dead people after they've passed, whether it's a relative or a good friend. I think the vibration may be just a little bit different right when people pass over. Like when an aunt or uncle has passed, I'll see them for a split moment.

And reading and studying metaphysical literature and many, many that say the same. The coolest thing that's happened—well, it was the worst thing in my life when David died, we'd been together for 22, 23 years, working together and living together. And he died very unexpectedly. And then this medium contacted me, Janice Carlson. She said she was willing to be the bridge, the telephone, for David. He wanted to document life after death, and he wanted to continue his column, an amazing development. So that was pretty cool.

Wow, I mean I was really in a bad way emotionally for a long time and that was . . . I mean I'd talked to a number of different mediums and it was kind of spontaneous. Nothing that I really sought out. Really just sort of people that I ran across. And that brought me a lot of comfort. David was such an unassuming, low key, mellow person. How could anyone be scared of him as a spirit? He was like an old shoe. But he was absolutely brilliant. And I hear him directly myself sometimes. He'll speak a little phrase or something. For instance, it was Christmas time and I was feeling kind of blue and sorry for myself and I was going to listen to some Pavarotti, the opera singer, and the Vienna Boys Choir on Christmas Day. And then I could feel/hear David standing behind me in the kitchen by the stairs. And like a smart ass he says, "I saw Pavarotti." Like nanner, nanner, nanner. We were huge fans of Pavarotti. We saw

Fate #546, Volume 48, #9 Sep. 1995 the annual UFO issue.

him in person in Saint Paul. When he was alive, he was here because Saint Paul and Modena, are sister cities, the town in Italy where he lived. David introduced me to opera. 'Course Motzart was his favorite composer. But we loved Pavarotti so we listened to a lot of his music.

So that was pretty cool. It was not like any sort of cosmic kind of thing. It was just like "I saw Pavarotti." Like he's still performing in spirit. So it's just many, many little things like this that has made me more comfortable with it.

TDE: Who or what inspires your work?

PG: I think probably all the readers of *Fate*. We get a lot of feedback from what they like and what they don't like. So I try to act like a steward of *Fate*. It's like I don't decide what goes in the magazine, somebody somewhere puts the information in front of me. Like we'll get three articles on bigfoot. Oh, I guess we better write about

September 2002

FATE

Free Reports of the Strange and Unknown

Terrifying Alien Abductions!

KGB & the Occult
Foo Fighters
Remote Sensing Results

Fate #629, Volume 55, #8 Sep. 2002
magazine-size with Robert Crumb cover.

bigfoot in this issue. So it seems to come in on some other dimension or channel. And I try to listen and be quiet, and centered, and pay attention to the types of articles that come in to us, over the Internet, or via letters. Or people will ask . . . it's kind of like a general wavelength that we try to pay attention to.

[Phyllis hears a sound downstairs in her house.] Oh gee, my snake just crashed and fell. I'm going to walk downstairs, I hope I don't loose you on this phone. I have a six-foot red tailed boa. She gets to get out and crawl around downstairs, on the shelving. Sounds like she might have gone crash. [pause] Ah, she's just knocking stuff down, she's fine. She's up there reading philosophy. [laughter]

TDE: The cover style and even the format of the magazine has changed over the years. What can you tell us about that?

PG: It started out as a pulp magazine. That's what the paper was like in the late '40s, on science fiction magazines. It was inexpensive to print on that kind of paper. And it pretty much stayed black-and-white during much of its 63-, 65-year career. Then it went full size, full color when Llewellyn had it. I believe that was in 1994. [June 1994 through April 2003] The Marketing person at Llewellyn thought it would be more desirable on the newsstand. It was strictly to attract more advertising and to be competitive on the newsstands.

After like ten years . . . I was agin' it, I didn't approve of that, in fact I quit when they decided to do that. I was the editor in the early '90s. Seemed like the wrong thing to do, change its personality. So it stayed that way with Llewellyn. So when they sold it to me, I changed it back to the digest size. Because people really preferred the digest size. It has its own personality and all the little old ladies can put it in their purse, go to the doctor's office, carry it around, or read it in bed.

TDE: What is your editorial planning process like?

PG: In the past, it was kind of themes. Like December was the spirituality kind of theme issue because it's Christmas. And October for the Fall was kind Halloweenish and ghosts, kind of things. September was UFO, and summertime we had archeology and nature spirit things.

We had a tough time economically when everything else in this country went to heck, with many magazines and newspapers going out of print. And then David leaving the planet. I had kind of a struggle, but now it's a little more spontaneous. Actually I have the next two or three issue cover ideas planned out.

We usually have a pretty good slush fund of articles that we have and we have professionals that we call on to write too. It's shorter term now, not so rigid as to what we have planned. Like the next issue cover will have Sasquatch on it. The one after that is personal experiences and the one after that is gonna be steampunk.

That will be kinda fun and I'm toying with tattoos, tattooed people in history and then my interns, they really want us to do one on doomsday prep. I'm not so fond of that, but they're younger and I try to be open minded. So *Fate* kind of writes itself. That's the best way that I can explain it.

TDE: Your articles cover a wide, wide range of topics. How do you find all this material?

PG: Our readers have consistently indicated that they like variety. Sometimes we have tried to do like mostly UFO kinds of related stories, but they get mad. Well, there's no ghosts in there. So to try to please everybody we try to get a little bit of everything in there. And because of the amount of submissions we get we can have that variety. We get a lot of unsolicited submissions. We try to choose something from several different topics for each issue.

I write my column and I just influence the rest of it. I hear tell that back in the day, when *Fate* first started, that Ray Palmer would write the whole thing under a whole bunch of different pseudonyms. The very first, maybe dozen issues or so they wouldn't have a lot of different writers and would just change names.

TDE: You offer *Fate* in multiple formats. What percentage of your subscribers are digital and print?

PG: At this point, maybe five percent are digital. It's pretty small but I think we'll see more and more digital subscribers. The core of our subscribers are mature people. Some of them don't even have a computer. We really have to answer to them and make sure they have what they want. They cling to the magazine, they say they can't live without their *Fate*. They wait until it comes and they read it cover to cover. So it's very important to them spiritually. It's kind of like their spiritual fix, because it's nondenominational and open-minded and objective.

We had to have it available, and we're getting more e-subscribers, but the bulk of our readers are older people and they like having something physical in front of them. And I personally can't stand to read a book on Kindle. I like to have something paper in front of me. It's just more tactile.

TDE: I haven't been able to find *Fate* on the newsstand in Portland, Oregon. Is distribution a challenge?

PG: Yes, it sure is. Our big distributor went bankrupt a couple years ago. Then Ingram took over all distribution for Barnes & Noble and they won't take any more digest-size magazines. So we're going to have some people doing gorilla marketing. If they want to see *Fate* in their favorite bookstore, ask for the store manager and buyer to carry it.

Our contact at Ingram wanted to carry *Fate* because she knew our sell through would be fabulous. But they were overwhelmed with being dumped on with all the magazines when the other distributor closed. That said, we do have other distributors who have taken up *Fate* again. So I'll see what we have out in Portland, and we'll put it up on our website, which stores will have *Fate*.

TDE: What sorts of things are you doing to grow sales and subscriptions?

PG: We had a series of interns sending out renewal notices so we're getting much more on top of that now. And we're attending more metaphysical/paranormal conferences. We're getting digital compilations of the best of *Fate* stories. We have a partner out in Berkley, California who is digitizing a lot of assortments of *Fate*. And then we're offering specials on our website. We're dropping the price dramatically for individual issues, and offering complete years.

I had some help, and in retrospect I'm sorry I listened to them, and we put the *Fates* at like $25 a piece, and that's crazy in this economy. Nobody can afford that. So we're going to drop prices across the board. And also the warehouse where we house our *Fate* is being sold by the landlord because he can't make a go of the building. And it leaks too, so in order to not have to move thousands and thousands of magazines we're going to do some inventory reduction with these special sales.

TDE: You offer posters and trading cards of past covers in the *Fate* magazine Store. What other plans do you have for merchandizing?

PG: We used to do T-shirts. Maybe we'll do T-shirts again with that first cover of *Fate*. And we also were gonna do a framed, high-quality print of the cover. Like in a wooden frame. Oh, and we've also done calendars in the past and we might do them again. And we're planning to do a coffee table book with some of the beauti-

ful, old classic cover art. So that's coming up probably next year.

TDE: How do you use social media to complement the magazine?

PG: To create interest and to create a community. I'm not as conversant in all of the social media as some of my younger helpers, so they are very sharp and it's just fun for people to read all kinds of things on Facebook, strange bits of stories and information we come up with.

We're starting Fate Radio here in the next week or two also. We'll have live Fate Radio and then the shows will be archived on our website.

TDE: What are a few of the highlights during your time as editor of *Fate*?

PG: I've gotten a chance to meet some really great people. And everywhere you go people recognize *Fate* magazine. It's just really nice to be associated with the entity of *Fate* that has such a wonderful reputation.

I was at Dragon Con down in Atlanta, Georgia one year. And stood in line to get my poster autographed. They were giving away free posters, Michael Whelan did this dragon poster, and there was a line out the door to see him, because he's an incredible fantasy artist. I mean it's like $20,000 for one of his paintings. So I just sort of shyly stood in line to get my poster autographed and handed him a couple issues of *Fate* magazine and he said, "Oh, *Fate* magazine. I used to read it when I was in high school. Went to the library to read it." I mean it's just like instant connection. It was so cool that he was like the rockstar of the fantasy artists world and here he was impressed to meet me as the editor of *Fate*.

And yeah, just meeting so

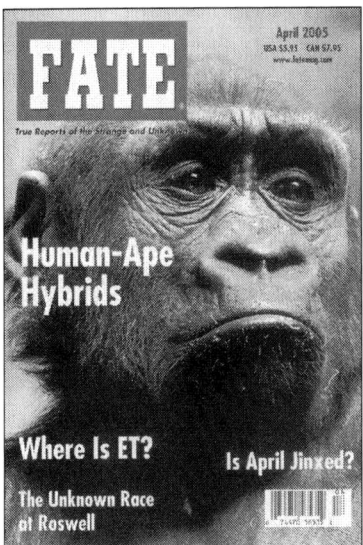

Fate #660, Volume 58, #4 Apr. 2005 with editor and publisher Phyllis Galde and managing editor David F. Godwin.

many people through the years. It's always a kick. "Yeah, I read *Fate* magazine." I mean everybody seems to be familiar with it when they were growing up, because it was the only game in town.

TDE: What's in store for *Fate* and your publishing company in 2015?

PG: I think things will be much smoother and more consistent— more exciting. I'm getting my feet back under me after losing David. That was a hell of a shock after, you know we worked together for so many years, we were just like a well-matched team of horses. So that really threw me for a loop. There was no warning. It was just such a total shock. So yeah, and I have some wonderful helpers now. Good energy and good guidance, and David is helping with spirit.

TDE: Thank you for sharing a few minutes with us. Are there any other comments you'd like to add?

PG: You always have a free e-issue available on the website. And if your readers write to us, we'll certainly send them a recent sample issue. And it's very reasonable to advertise in *Fate*.

This is kinda cool, we get historically, like a million hits on our website every month. I haven't checked the Google analytics lately, but I think it's kinda cool that we get a lot of people from the military that are following our site. I don't know if they're bored in their jobs, or if they're following us for conspiracy stuff, which is not a big part of the magazine. But I thought that was kind of interesting. Kind of surprised me.

So it's a good place for people to advertise their wares, because our rates are extremely reasonable. We have people who've advertised with *Fate*—not since it started, because they probably aren't still alive, but for years and years and years. Regular advertising until they are no longer around. We get results. It's a very special little entity. It has its own oversoul, guardian spirit if you will. And we appreciate your support.

And I've got somebody in mind to carry on *Fate* when I decide to retire too.

Subscribe to *Fate* at fatemag.com
6 mo. e-edition sub. $9.95
6 mo. print sub. $14.95
6 mo. print sub. deluxe mailing $20.95
1 yr. e-edition sub. $19.95
1 yr. print sub. $27.95
1 yr. print sub. with deluxe mailing $39.95
2 y.r e-edition sub. $36.95
2 yr. print sub. $53.95
2 yr. print sub. with deluxe mailing $77.95

Full years of original *Fate* magazines:
1965–1969 $59.95 each
1970, 1972–1979 $49.95 each
1980–1987, 1989 $44.95 each

Fate #725
Review by Rudolph Schmidt

From the masthead: "*Fate* magazine has featured 'True Reports of the Strange and Unknown' since 1948. *Fate* is the longest-running periodical in its field and the only one to offer readers a compelling mix of factual documentation, exclusive investigative reporting, and real personal experiences serving to expand awareness, fire the imagination, and enrich lives."

As readers since the early '50s have come to expect, "I See by the Papers" is *Fate*'s opening ingress. A series of outré news briefs that immediately orient newcomers and warm up regulars for a journey into the fantastic. In this particular outing, topics range from "Pet Cemeteries Now Accepting Human Remains" in New York (ashes only) to "Ouija Board Sends Three People to Hospital in Mexico?"

If your fascination centers on a specific interest, perhaps ghosts or alien abduction, you're likely find an article that resonates in every issue. For spiritualists, in this edition, renown psychic, spiritual healer and teacher Echo Bodine shares the very personal story of her mother's passing and later visita-tions. "I'm so grateful to know the soul continues on after death," she writes. And for ufologists, Ardy Sixkiller Clarke interviews several eye witnesses to the aliens among us in "An Encounter in Alaska."

If you're a generalist, you'll find even more to enjoy. *Fate*'s stories are short and crisp, four to twelve pages each. Many are first-hand accounts of strange encounters. Others are well researched historical reports. All are illustrated with relevant photographic evidence, if available.

In this issue's "From the Editor," Phyllis Galde shares her latest adventures swimming with dolphins in the Caribbean, her thoughts about the issue, and *Fate*'s new numbering scheme. "Because our printing schedule has been somewhat irregular, and the calendar date does not match the current publication, we will now refer to *Fate* by the sequential number on the front [#725]."

What follows is a brief overview of the balance of the issue, with the intension to provide only enough information for an accurate impression. The digest is easy enough to purchase via subscription from fatemag.com, but may not be readily available to browse at your local newsstand. The website also offers a free sample e-issue, but of course the experience in print is superior.

The issue's cover story, "Dolphins Speak to Us!" is a succession of three transcriptions. First, Penelope Smith, a pioneer in animal communication and founding editor of *Species Link* magazine, translates a dolphin's message to mankind. The cetacean mammal unleashes a bombshell: dolphins are interdimensional beings. This revelation is followed by advice from a bottle nose dolphin, and a captive dolphin from the Dominican Republic, reported to us respectively by Cyndie Lepori and Madeleine Walker.

"Final Requiem, the Hall-Mills Murders" by Katharine Clark is a true crime story. Circa 1922, Clark's absorbing research can't quite bring closure to the unsolved double murder of Rev. Edward Hall and Eleanor Mills, but her exploration of the evidence and the quirks of those involved, provide a fascinating read.

Paul Hogan discovers the "The Holy Men of Straw" in a remote village in Colombia. "There, I came across, arguably, the most amazing man I'd ever seen."

Cora Smilkovich recounts a brief encounter with an unusual creature, possibly supernatural, possibly alien, in "Chupacabras— A Cover Up Conspiracy?"

Barbara E. Lewter explores a new perspective on events from the 17th century in "Alien Abduction and the Salem Witch Trials."

Contributing editor and founder of *Tales From the Shadow Realm*, the fiction magazine of horror and suspense, Devlin Blake, explores strange events throughout the history of North Carolina's Outer Banks. Her report includes the disappearing hotel of Jockey's Ridge, the insanity of Theodosia Burr, and the miracle of Saint Andrews by the Sea.

Paranormal expert, Rosemary Ellen Guiley, compares the virtues of high tech tools and those of the body in "Paranormal Investigation." One of the tips she shares, "You can train your 'ghost vision' by practicing looking into space or the distance without focusing on any particular object. Pay attention to what comes into view in your peripheral vision."

Hidden at the top of a sheer ridge, high in the Himalayas, Lake Roopkund, is known by the locals as the "Mystery Lake." Retired editor and journalist, Chuck Lyons uncovers the facts in "What Happened at Skeleton Lake?"

Diane Tessman is the author of *The UFO Agenda*. In her *Fate* contribution, "UFOs and Ghosts," she posits a series of eight questions that seek a connection between the two seemingly alien entities.

In Native Americans' Nation of Spirits, ghosts are not haunting apparitions, they are Spirit Guides. First, Jessica Freeberg grounds readers with an origin story, "Wovoka and the Ghost Dance." Then, in "The Ghost Dance Returns," Janet Red Feather shares additional tribal history and the modern day meaning of the dance.

As interesting as much of this issue's reports are, the highlight is unmistakable. A reprint from December 1962, "Mark Twain's Mental Telegraphy," which was originally published in *Harper's*, December 1891. A nine-page report in which the renown author shares his personal experiences with what the Psychical Society of England named Telepathy.

Contributing Editor, Micah Hanks, provides part two of his "Beyond the Known" series. He brings his discussion of the animal world's capacity to communicate to the subject of dolphins, and their well-documented intelligence. Their understanding of ecosystems may go well beyond ours, as he presents further evidence of the interconnected world we share.

Readers gain the spotlight next. First, in the letters column, and then in a series of first-hand accounts of survival after death, reincarnation and ghostly visitations. If published, *Fate* pays $10 for readers' stories of their strange experiences.

Jerome Clark and the *Fate* staff's book reviews feature *Seeing Fairies* by Margarorie T. Johnson and *The Emperor's Stargate, Success On All Levels* by Albert Cheung Kwong Yin and Alexandra Harteam.

The former Managing Editor of *Fate*, David F. Godwin, passed away on October 16, 2012. Yet, his spirit is still in communication with the living. Medium Janice Carlson shared his observations about the afterlife with Phyllis Galde, which are featured on the closing page of the issue.

One of *Fate*'s ancillary pleasures are its advertisements. Although not as plentiful as years gone by, the issue includes ads of all sizes, including two pages of classifieds. Don't overlook them or contributors' biographical notes. You'll find lots to explore on the websites noted.

Fate #725's full color cover is printed on glossy stock of a serviceable weight. Interior pages are printed on a paper that could be described as high-quality newsprint. The outermost signature (first and last 16 pages) are full color. I suspect this is primarily done to boost ad revenue, as the final 16 pages are mostly ads. The rest of the magazine (120 pages total) are black-and-white. Production values are fair. The photography and gray-scale images inside are low contrast. Think deep gray, not black.

It could be that my subscription copy is an anomaly, but a few of the pages were clearly make-ready sheets, in printshop jargon, and the outermost text characters on several pages teetered on the edge of being cut off by the trim. The final size is 5-1/4" x 7-5/8" with saddle-stitch binding. $5.95 retail price.

One of the most unique digests still in print, *Fate* covers such a wide range of strange events and inexplicable phenomena, that anyone with even a glimmer of interest in the supernatural or mysterious is sure to enjoy it. Dive in at fatemag.com

Galaxy Science Fiction: The H.L. Gold Years

Article by Larry Johnson

Within five months of its debut in October 1950, *Galaxy Science Fiction* magazine was turning a profit—and within one year was outselling its competitor *Astounding*. A few years later it expanded to foreign editions and its stories were adapted into radio plays for the *X-Minus One* program.

This phenomenal success can be attributed to the efforts of editor H.L. Gold, who strove to elevate the standards of science fiction from the Buck Rogers/space opera days to stories about the effects of man's technology on society.

Horace L. Gold, a science fiction fan at a young age, began his career as a magazine writer and assistant editor in the 1930s. By the early 1940s, he was writing for DC Comics.

Illustration by Virgil Finlay for Robert Sheckley's *"The Native Problem"* (December 1956).

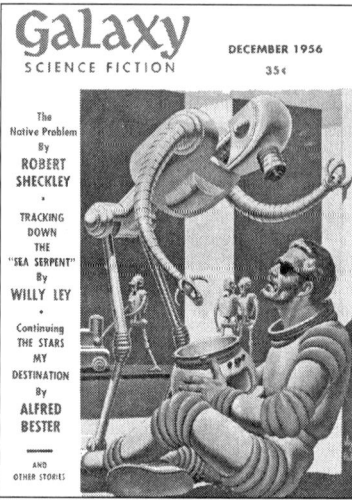

Galaxy
SCIENCE FICTION

DECEMBER 1956
35¢

The
Native Problem
By
ROBERT
SHECKLEY
·
TRACKING
DOWN
THE
"SEA SERPENT"
By
WILLY LEY
·
Continuing
THE STARS
MY
DESTINATION
By
ALFRED
BESTER
——
AND
OTHER STORIES

Cover by Virgil Finlay illustrating
"Help For Mankind."

This ambitious editor and imaginative writer, who spearheaded the groundbreaking *Galaxy* digest, suffered from agoraphobia due to his experiences in World War II, and confined himself to his apartment. There, over the phone and in meetings with visitors, he was able to gather a talented pool of writers for his magazine.

During its first decade *Galaxy* presented cutting edge work by authors such as Ray Bradbury (whose story "The Fireman" later expanded into *Fahrenheit 451*) and Damon Knight (whose "To Serve Man" was adapted into a memorable episode of *The Twilight Zone*).

C.M. Hornbluth, Alfred Bester, Brian Aldiss, Robert Sheckley, Curt Simak, Evelyn E. Smith, Isaac Asimov, William Tenn and a host of other notables in the science fiction field were all featured in those early issues.

Gold's exacting standards were exemplified in a story from an early issue, "Beyond Bedlam"

by author Wyman Guin (August 1951). This tale, which concerned a future society where schizophrenia is rampant and the population is required to take medication, was the result of two drafts before submission and two end-to-end rewrites afterwards. Gold stated in that issue's editorial: "If 'Beyond Bedlam' is not a good story, it isn't because author and editor did not sweat bullets to make it so."

This caliber of editing and honing of intriguing concepts was continued shortly thereafter with the publication of Alfred Bester's serialized novel *The Demolished Man* (January–February 1952). Gold had contacted Bester, at the time a successful radio scripter and fellow comic book writer alumni, for a contribution to his magazine. Initially the author suggested a scenario in the future where police were equipped with time machines in order to trace a crime back to its origin. Gold nixed that idea, informing Bester that time travel was a pretty worn out concept and suggested instead that he use ESP. In fact, the editor went on to insist that this story should take place in a future society where ESP is commonplace.

After much discussion and revision between editor and author the final product debuted. It was well received by *Galaxy* readers, and went on to become a bestselling book.

In an editorial in the March 1953 issue, the editor clearly stated the types of stories that prospective authors should *not* be submitting to *Galaxy*:

"Fictional warnings of nuclear and biological destruction, the post-atomic world, reversion to barbarism, mutant children slain

Galaxy

SCIENCE FICTION

MAY 1952
35¢

Cover by Jack Coggins titled "Mining an Asteroid."

because they have only ten toes and fingers instead of twelve, absurdly planned and preposterously successful revolts against dictatorships, problems of survival wearily turned over to women, war between groups, nations, worlds and solar systems.

"Flying Saucers, cops and robbers or cowboys and Indians in space, the duel between the good guy and the bad guy alone on an asteroid, the bright revelation that the characters we have been reading about are Adam and Eve or Jesus, the creation of a miniature universe in a laboratory by a scientist whose name turns out to be an anagram of Jehovah, the alien eater of life force in the Andes whose menu consists exclusively of pretty virgins."

Galaxy
SCIENCE FICTION

NOVEMBER 1954
35¢
ASTEROID ROUNDUP
By Willy Ley

Cover by Ed Emshwiller (EMSH) illustrating "Space-Time ı One Tough Lesson."

In that very same issue H.L. Gold's novella "The Old Die Rich" appeared. It dealt with time travel—a subject he had dissuaded Alfred Bester to pursue—but there was a unique twist to this tale. The plot involved a scheme to send people back 20 years in the past to make wise investments in the stock market. When they returned to the present they were well off financially but died from "malnutrition induced by senile psychosis." How come? It had something to do with the ingestion of food from another time, a unique element never dealt with before in the history of time travel fiction!

This story, by the way, was one of many from the magazine that was adapted into a radio play for the *X-Minus One* program.

"Hostess" by Isaac Asimov (May 1951) was another engaging tale to appear in the radio series. The story involved a couple hosting a cyanide breathing doctor from Hawkin's Planet with an interesting outcome. The consequences of society's

mores were not the only themes pursued in the pages of *Galaxy*. Natural disaster was the subject of Fritz Leiber's "A Pail of Air" (December 1951) (and it also was featured on *X-Minus One*). This was a poignant tale told from a child's point of view, concerning one family's efforts to survive on Earth after it was pulled into a new orbit around a "dark star" and all the oxygen froze. The family lived deep inside a city building, and survived by tending a fire fed by buckets of this "frozen air" brought in from the outside.

Leiber, with a background in theatre and encyclopedia writing, served as editor of *Science Digest* magazine, starting in 1947.

Gold recognized the need for a science column in *Galaxy* as well and hired Willy Ley, a German immigrant, to write "For Your Information" which debuted in the March 1952 issue. Ley was involved in the German Rocket Society in the 1920s and served as technical advisor for the films *Woman in the Moon* and *Metropolis*.

His first column focused on astronomy and contained readers' science questions. More space related columns ensued, including space travel and the development of a space station. Other topics such as dinosaurs, mathematics, ancient civilizations and hoaxes followed. His wife Olga provided illustrations for these columns, specializing in lively depictions of prehistoric animals.

Reader queries ranged from "How does the H-Bomb work?" to math questions, to the legend of Atlantis and zoological oddities; always answered with Ley's unique flair.

Although there was a share of dramatic stories in *Galaxy*, some-

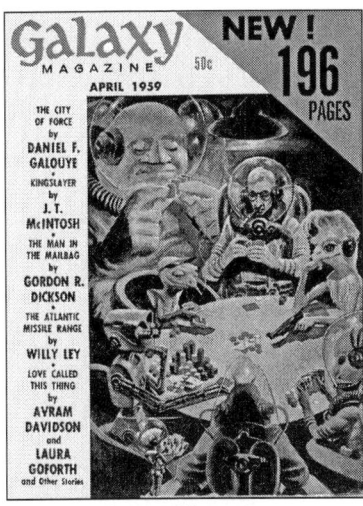

Cover by Wally Wood illustrating
"A Full House Beats Togetherness."

Illustration by Don Martin for Thomas N.
Scortia's "The Bomb in the Bathtub."

times more lighthearted fare was also featured. One such story, "Lulu" written by Clifford Simak (June 1957), fit this bill perfectly. Dealing with what we would now refer to as "artificial intelligence" Lulu was the name given to a computerized system running a space ship with an overly-developed motherly instinct for her three human charges. This delightful tale was abetted by some very amusing illustrations by Don Martin of *Mad Magazine* fame. Yes, his goofy looking, floppy-footed people were on full display.

Artificial intelligence was also the theme of another Simak-penned tale entitled "How-2" (November 1954). The plot involved a man who had ordered a robot dog kit from the How-2 Corporation. By mistake, he received an experimental robot named Albert that promptly created scores and scores of specialized robots to improve the man's yard and house. The legal and ethical ramifications of this arrangement made for engaging reading and

the accompanying art made the story even more entertaining.

"How-2" was illustrated by an artist who went by the "pen name" EMSH, one of many talented artists employed by *Galaxy* during this period (including, among others, Wally Wood and Virgil Finlay). Ed Emshwiller had the knack for applying a different style to practically every story he illustrated—from pen and ink work, to airbrush, to scratchboard technique, to pencil, to paint—and his depiction of the characters and action in the stories was always accurate.

In fact, his first commercial work appeared on the cover of *Galaxy* for the June 1951 issue. Many covers ensued, including imaginative Christmas issues featuring an alien four-armed Santa Claus.

Another EMSH-illustrated story, "Collector's Item" by Evelyn E. Smith (December 1954), was a witty tale about an expedition of scientists in search of zoological specimens on Venus. The group

Cover by EMSH offering "Seasons Greetings to Our Readers."

Cover by Jack Gaughan illustrating "Salvage From 50,000,000 B.C."

slogs through the steamy jungles of the planet led by a supposedly native guide in the story. The belief that Venus may have harbored a type of life under its cloud layer was in the realm of possibility at the time.

"Drunkard's Walk," a two-part serial by Frederick Pohl (June–August 1960) was in a more serious vein. It focused on a university mathematics professor who was obsessed with making repeated suicidal attempts by flinging himself from a great height, slashing his throat and taking an overdose of sleeping pills. No psychological reason is proven. Instead there is an elaborate plot by an elite class of beings hellbent on killing off their lesser human brethren by the use of a virus.

This type of "thinking man's story" is indicative of the speculative fiction Galaxy championed under H.L. Gold's editorship. Pohl, at the time, served as assistant editor and, after Gold was severely injured in a taxi cab accident that year, took over the position of editor of the magazine for the next decade.

Under Frederick Pohl's guidance Galaxy continued to excel in publishing even more cutting edge stories, paving the way for the new wave of science fiction in the 1960s. This standard of excellence, of course, was directly due to the efforts of the magazine's founding editor H.L. Gold. He brought a "sophisticated intellectual subtlety" to magazine science fiction, according to Pohl, and "after Galaxy it was impossible to go on being naive."

Galaxy Science Fiction magazine was a game changer. Its effect on the genre can be felt to this day. ✒

Larry Johnson has published the small press comic book, *Tales of Fantasy*, for over 25 years. A member of the United Fanzine Organization, landscape painter, science fiction fan, SF digest collector, and a life long comics creator who teaches the craft at a local art center. His book *The Best of Tales of Fantasy* is available on Amazon. Visit him online at LarryJohnsonartist.com

Digest 911:
Digest Protection—Sleeves

By D. Blake Werts
Technical assistance from Denae Horneman

If you spend any time at all with me and any of my hobbies, you'll soon learn that I'm quite obsessive about the preservation/protection of my collectibles. Yes, I'm one of those types that sincerely believes he is merely the custodian during my time on this planet. As such, I consider it my "duty" to protect said collectible before it gets passed along to a new "owner." So it should be no surprise that I've spent quite a bit of time searching for suitable sleeves to store my digest collection.

Among the various offerings ClearBags (www.clearbags.com) makes available for a wide range of industries, they have a line of bags, or "sleeves" as I call them, made

out of a superb archival material called "BOPP." Biaxially-Oriented Polypropylene (BOPP) is superior to many packaging materials due to its strength, flatness, clarity and light weight. BOPP's optical properties, the transparency and shine of the material, are among the best available. The strength of BOPP is noted through its puncture, bursting, and tear resistance. More importantly, BOPP also has a very high stability/performance over a wide range of environmental conditions. It also has a high resistance to chemicals (fat/oils). And likely the most important quality, BOPP is food grade with archival qualities.

I've used ClearBags sleeves

for a number of years now and can attest to many of the qualities mentioned. From this experience, I won't hesitate to recommend their line of "Crystal Clear Bags" for any of your collectibles, especially when it comes to digests and magazines. Lucky for us, ClearBags offers a wide range of sleeve sizes which proves to be a blessing when it comes finding that nice, snug fit for nearly any dimensions.

I prefer to use sleeves that provide a snug fit. Not only does this help give added protection to the digest, it also prevents the digest from slipping around inside of the sleeve while handling/shelving the digest. A snug fit also helps keep the collection looking a bit more tidy. Additionally, if there is a "Protective Closure" option available (adhesive strip on the bag and not the flap), I will choose that option. Otherwise the adhesive seal is placed on the flap ("Flap Seal") which could get caught on the digest cover when removing it from the sleeve.

The chart on the facing page presents my sleeve recommendations arranged more-or-less by size.

The first column is the size of the digest in Width x Height x Thickness format. The second column simply notes an example digest title from which the measurement was taken. And the third column is the ClearBags product ID followed by the product specs. If there are two options provided, this simply means that there is both a Protective Closure and a Flap Seal option available—choose the style that best fits your needs.

I should point out that Clear-Bags is happy to provide samples of any of their sleeves upon request. This is a superb way to test your own item dimensions if you aren't able to locate a close match from the chart on the adjacent page, or if you would like to see how the sleeves perform before making a commitment on a substantial order.

I'm from the future and I'm here to check
on the accuracy of your predictions.

W x H x T	Digest Title	ClearBags Number (W x H)
4 7/8" x 6 5/8" x 1/4"	Archie 2014 regular	B6B1PC (5 5/16" x 6 3/4")
4 7/8" x 6 5/8" x 3/8"	Archie 2014 double	B6B1PC (5 5/16" x 6 3/4") S
4 7/8" x 6 5/8" x 1/2"	Archie 2014 jumbo	B75PC (5 7/16" x 7 1/4")
4 7/8" x 6 11/16" x 5/16"	Archie 1975	B75PC (5 7/16" x 7 1/4")
5 1/8" x 7 5/8" x 3/4"	F&SF 2014	BA5SPC (6 1/16" x 8 3/8")
		BA5S (6 1/16" x 8 3/8") S
5 1/8" x 7 7/16" x 5/16"	Asimov's 1990s	B7B2PC (5 13/16" x 7 1/2")
		B75XL (5 7/8" x 7 3/4")
5 1/8" x 7 7/16" x 5/16"	Analog 1990s	B7B2PC (5 13/16" x 7 1/2")
		B75XL (5 7/8" x 7 3/4")
5 3/16" x 7 1/4" x 5/16"	Readers Digest 2014	B7B2PC (5 13/16" x 7 1/2")
5 3/16" x 7 5/8" x 1/2"	Galaxy 1973	B5N9PC (5 15/16" x 7 3/4")
		B75XL (5 7/8" x 7 3/4")
5 3/16" x 7 9/16" x 3/8"	Mike Shayne 1976	B5N9PC (5 15/16" x 7 3/4")
		B75XL (5 7/8" x 7 3/4")
5 3/16" x 7 5/8" x 9/16"	F&SF 1974	B5N9PC (5 15/16" x 7 3/4")
		B75XL (5 7/8" x 7 3/4")
5 5/16" x 7 1/4" x 1/4"	Coronet 1955	B7B2PC (5 13/16" x 7 1/2")
5 1/4" x 7 3/16" x 1/4"	Startling Mystery	B75PC (5 7/16" x 7 1/4")
		B75 (5 7/16" x 7 1/4") S
5 1/4" x 7 1/2" x 5/16"	F&SF 1973	B7B2PC (5 13/16" x 7 1/2")
		B75XL (5 7/8" x 7 3/4")
5 1/4" x 7 1/2" x 3/8"	Ellery Queen 1972	B7B2PC (5 13/16" x 7 1/2")
		B75XL (5 7/8" x 7 3/4")
5 1/4" x 7 1/2" x 3/8"	Short Story Intl. '92	B7B2PC (5 13/16" x 7 1/2")
		B75XL (5 7/8" x 7 3/4")
5 1/4" x 7 5/8" x 3/8"	Espionage	B75XL (5 7/8" x 7 3/4")
5 3/8" x 7 1/4" x 5/16"	Imagination 1954	B7B2PC (5 13/16" x 7 1/2")
5 3/8" x 7 5/8" x 5/16"	IF	B75XL (5 7/8" x 7 3/4")
5 3/8" x 7 5/8" x 3/8"	Analog 1969	B5N9PC (5 15/16" x 7 3/4")
		B75XL (5 7/8" x 7 3/4")
5 3/8" x 7 5/8" x 7/16"	Analog 1979	B5N9PC (5 15/16" x 7 3/4")
		B75XL (5 7/8" x 7 3/4")
5 3/8" x 7 5/8" x 1/4"	The Big Story	B7B2PC (5 13/16" x 7 1/2")
		B75XL (5 7/8" x 7 3/4")
5 7/16" x 7 7/16" x 1/8"	Hello Buddies 1945	B7B2PC (5 13/16" x 7 1/2")
		B75XL (5 7/8" x 7 3/4") L
5 7/16" x 7 5/8" x 3/16"	Fate 2008	B7B2PC (5 13/16" x 7 1/2")
		B75XL (5 7/8" x 7 3/4") L
5 1/2" x 7 3/8" x 5/16"	Fate 1969	B7B2PC (5 13/16" x 7 1/2")
		B75XL (5 7/8" x 7 3/4") S
5 1/2" x 7 5/8" x 5/16"	F&SF 1949	B7B2PC (5 13/16" x 7 1/2")
		B75XL (5 7/8" x 7 3/4")
5 1/2" x 8 1/2" x 5/16"	Grift 2012	B59PC (5 15/16" x 8 3/4")
5 7/8" x 8 1/2" x 1/4"	Analog 2014 regular	B68HPC (6 1/4" x 8 1/2") BF
		B6X9 (6 7/16" x 9") L
5 7/8" x 8 1/2" x 1/2"	Analog 2014 double	B6X9 (6 7/16" x 9")

S=Snug L=Loose BF=Best Fit

A Darker Night

Fiction by Joe Wehrle, Jr.

"How are you named?" asked Elk.

"Firefly." She rode proudly in the saddle, despite her bedraggled appearance, her tangled orange hair.

"Is there any water?" she asked.

"None," Raven answered. She looked down at the sleeping Xeenaarl, cradled in her arms as she rode. "When he recovers, he'll lead us to water. It should be soon."

"I have him to thank for my life . . . and both of you as well. Many would have traveled on. He . . . he drove the raiders' mounts away . . . with his mind?"

Raven nodded. "Yes. And he's exhausted."

They rode on through the morning until the flecks of sunlight fell from directly above. The Xeenaarl roused himself and indicated the direction in which water could be found. He did not know this instinctively, but ascertained his facts from stray animal thoughts he picked up.

The waterhole lay in the midst of a grove of tall, thin arko trees. They approached cautiously, but the Xeenaarl showed no alarm, only eagerness. Of the humans, Raven first spotted the creature drinking there and cautioned the others against a closer approach.

It was incredibly long-legged and long-necked and bore itself with dignity. Long streaks of white fur ran the length of its back, down to the short, tufted tail. Its major color was brown, but a graduated brown which darkened almost to black at the toed feet, lightened almost to cream at the face. The animal continued to drink for a short time, then lifted its shapely head and looked apprehensively in their direction. Sensing their presence, it turned and gracefully slipped into the dense foliage.

The four watchers came to the hole then and drank their fill. Elk refilled the waterskins while the young women watched the Xeenaarl lapping water with his rough tongue. Firefly removed her torn and dirty outer garment and washed herself in the pool. Raven was watching Elk closely so he pretended not to be interested.

In her traveling pack Raven found a serviceable woven tunic for Firefly, while she herself changed into a dark blue riding outfit which contrasted favorably with her even darker hair and added a new note to her deep green eyes. She brushed the dust from her bark-hide boots with a bit of bristly shrub she had pulled.

As they sat by the waterhole, a thin figure emerged from between the trees on the other side. Firefly shrank back as she recognized Eihkarradi features, but Raven glanced over at Elk to see if her suspicion was correct.

Elk stood and raised his hand in greeting.

"Seeker! It is you! Don't worry about this one, Firefly." The witchman came around the waterhole and sat. The talisman on his finger was dark, suggesting none of his brethren likely to be in the vicinity.

"I see you've added a member to your party," he said, scrutinizing Firefly from her orange hair down to her small, bruised bare feet. She stared back at him venomously.

Elk described their rescue of the young woman. "I didn't expect to see you again," he said.

"I wander near, and I wander far," the Eihkarrad replied cryptically. "There are many places I call home, known to none but me. Not even to the others who wear this ring." He brandished it. "I believe we're all going in the same direction. If you're agreeable, I'd like to ride with you."

"You're welcome to," Elk told him. "Our animals can easily bear your weight."

They mounted the two eloeir and proceeded on their way.

Firefly sat as far behind the witch-man as she could without tumbling off the eloeir's rump.

They rode 'til nightfall, the forest supplying what food they required. When they camped, Raven and Elk rolled up together in a borka covering, giving their second one to Firefly. Seeker slept in the fork of a tree, as was his custom on the trail.

Raven was awakened by the excited Xeenaarl. She thought it was still night, for it was fairly dark, but it was a sort of flickering kind of dark. Alarmed, she shook Elk. He pulled himself up. Still waking, and tried to understand what was happening. They heard the flap of wings. It sounded as if some creatures—some things—were massing around them. Seeker dropped down from his tree.

"What is it?" Elk asked.

The witchman looked more hollow-eyed than ever. "I've heard of these things," he said. "Some call them shrouds. They're symbionts; huge leather-winged flying creatures—carnivorous, but too awkward to do their own hunting—allied with fat, evil little fanged things, excellent killers, but they can tolerate no light, not even the light of the moon. Not even the dying embers of a fire."

Elk looked around quickly, then remembered that they hadn't hung up the small energy lamp when they bedded down, as the light might disturb Firefly, who desperately needed a sound night's sleep. It was tied to one of the eloeir, trained and untethered for its safety beyond the grove of trees within which they camped.

"The small creatures live within dark, pouchlike folds in the flying beasts' bellies," Seeker continued, speaking quickly. "The fliers encircle their prey and fly against the trees, overlapping wings tightly. When they're finished, the prey is entrapped in an inky black cage, leathery wings spread from the branches above to the ground around the trees. Then the fat little killers creep from their pouches and attack. There is usually no escape."

The darkness grew inexorably. Raven tried to get the Xeenaarl to drive the creatures off, but they were either too intent of purpose or possessed of nervous systems too alien to be vulnerable to his mental probings. Elk tied dry reeds to a broken branch, fashioning a torch which he lit with a spark from his pocket flint.

"If they've sealed us from the air, we can't hope to keep a fire going," he said, but we need time to think!"

Raven looked around her. The circle was complete, the torch just a temporary protection, and the focused, stunning beams from their sun-powered weapons would not be very effective against massed attackers. Even if they killed some of the winged things, their carcasses would still remain locked in suffocating tent formation, allowing their symbionts to attack in the dark.

Elk hesitantly approached the wall of wings. He thrust the torch before him, holding it against the rough gray wall. The burned wing was drawn back with a jerk, then replaced with a quick flap that extinguished the torch.

Elk fumbled again for his flint as a rustling came from above. He feared it was over for them. Then the torch caught.

He joined the others and they sat together, thoughts racing. They were besieged.

Seeker pulled at some reeds absent-mindedly. As he examined them more closely, he leaped to his feet.

"If you can keep that torch burning a little longer, Elk, I think we might yet survive!

"Look at these plants. They do not grow in soil. The only substance that nourishes them is Narbekian sponge-moss."

"Which grows several feet deep," said Elk, beginning to understand. He and the witchman drew their sharp knives and began to cut a large rectangular outline through the tough crust. Seeker lifted a corner and they proceeded to peel the crust away like a large, thick mat.

Raven and Firefly fashioned a second torch while they worked. The air was still good.

They set the mat aside and began tearing out great chunks of gray-green spongy stuff, moving as quickly as possible. While Raven held the torches, Firefly disposed of the mossy chunks, scattering them here and there in the reeds under the trees. Then the four of them along with the Xeenaarl climbed into the hole and positioned themselves. Elk, holding the last torch, climbed out as soon as he had seen that everyone fit inside the cavity. He dragged the thick top layer over the others and slipped under it himself, holding his torch outside one corner.

"Make sure all edges are down tight!"

"I think the cover's in place," Raven said, anxiously. "It seems like a perfect fit." She tested by pushing against the mat, but the porous material adhered tightly to itself. Elk extinguished the torch and yanked his corner down tight.

"How can they know when it's dark?" Firefly whispered.

"It's said that the fleshy pouches relax in total darkness," Seeker replied. "Now, hush!"

There came faint rustling sounds above now, and a sort of breathy sniffing. They tried not to move at all, each wondering how long the air would last. But the spongy material around them seemed to exude air.

Sharp claws scraped and yanked at the cover, but its size and the tenacity of the moss held it securely. Now they heard terrible wails and the rustling grew to a feverish tempo. Small bodies thrashed, screaming and raking the moss.

After a time it was quiet. Then they heard the beating of great wings, and they knew the creatures had gone. Not in silent, gliding fashion as when they had come to entrap, but throbbing away above the trees in futile, madly-despairing flight.

Joe Wehrle, Jr. is a writer and artist. He published the prized indie Big Little Book *Cauliflower Catnip Pearls of Peril* in 1981. His stories and artwork have appeared in the *Menomonee Falls Gazette*, 1971 *Clarion* Anthology, *Vampirella*, *Two-Gun Raconteur*, *Worlds of If*, *Galaxy* and many other publications. For more of his bibliography visit MidnightFiction.com/about/wehrle6.htm

Larque Press News

For periodic updates about *The Digest Enthusiast* and other Larque Press projects send your email address to

Arkay@larquepress.com

We will not share your email or send any messages other than updates on *The Digest Enthusiast* and news of other books or projects from Larque Press.

Coronet June 1950
Review by David Burnette

When I have a digest in hand, more often than not, it will be a genre-related publication, usually science fiction/fantasy, though I've been known to enjoy some mystery/detective fiction from time to time. And when I'm really looking for something nostalgic, I reach for one of the many "general interest" titles that were popular in the 1950s and 1960s. One such title that satisfies my tastes is *Coronet*.

Owned by *Esquire*, *Coronet* began publication in October 1936 and ended its 299-issue run in March 1971. Until 1961, *Coronet* was published by David A. Smart. Borrowing from Wikipedia, "Each issue had a wide variety of articles and features, as well as a condensed book section. Poetry was featured, along with gift advice and star stories. The sister company Coronet Films was promoted in most issues as well. Articles on culture and the arts were mixed with adventure stories and social advice." *Coronet* seemed to be targeted to both men and women.

My most recent *Coronet* read

was the June 1950 issue edited by Gordon Carroll. Coming off a binge of science fiction, this became a refreshing treat. In fact, I do wish we still had a digest title like this on our shelves today. True, the makeup of *Reader's Digest* is close, though missing an important component I think, that made *Coronet* the well-rounded package it once was—some good fiction stories.

Some non-fiction highlights from this issue include a really left-of-center leaning feature, "The Water Shortage Menaces America." Reporting on events in the late 1940s and where the country is headed, the piece comes off pretty strong in terms of reminding readers that better choices need to be made on water usage. Being somewhat of a tree-hugger, I found myself applauding the author throughout the article. There's also an article about birth control, how it can't help family planning without some real changes in education, "Birth Control is Not Enough." Birth control openly discussed in 1950? And one more that I'll mention, another "get your act together America" article, about the completely insane Coroner "office" we have in the US (and for many counties in the southeast, I can tell you this *is still* a major problem), "The Coroner Racket: A National Scandal."

In terms of fiction, there are bits of mystery/detective, some "feel-good" stories, and the piece that drove me to seek this particular issue out, a Ray Bradbury short entitled "They Landed On Mars." 100% of the fiction proved to be enjoyable reads.

Of course the digest included some great advertising from the period, cars, electronics, and even a beautiful full page ad for Sawyer's View Master! And a couple of "photo features"—think black and white *National Geographic* on a lesser quality paper stock—just a hair better than the true pulp paper the text features are printed on. The 175-page issue featured a splendid cover painting by Geoffrey Biggs entitled "Foot-loose and Fancy Free."

For completeness, the table of contents lists the following:

Articles and *Fiction:

Pictorial Features:

Departments:

Book Features:
Birth Control is Not Enough
When the Navy Held a "Schmootzle"

I'd say about a third of the material was previously published elsewhere, with the rest, presumably, original material for *Coronet*. The only shortcoming I had with the issue, and maybe this is the norm for the title, is that many of the articles and stories were only three or four pages, or less. I'd prefer a few longer pieces in the mix.

Another thing that made this issue such an enjoyable read to me was the mere fact that it was the product of some type of letterpress process. For me, letterpress printing is so much easier and more enjoyable to read, especially when you've got good sunlight to help the "bite" of each letter reveal itself in three dimensions on the page. Even with the illustrations, most were well-executed line-illustrations with a single color "wash" background. Gorgeous to look at!

So if you are in the mood for some "general interest" reading, or want to take a time-capsule back to some 1950's nostalgia, I strongly recommend giving *Coronet* a close look. They can be easily acquired through the normal online outlets, and often at bargain prices. I think you'll be surprised—they are a lot of fun.

Science doesn't want you to donate your body
to them. Want to try science fiction?

Gordon Van Gelder

Interview with F&SF's editor and publisher.
By D. Blake Werts

When Arkay asked me to reach out to Gordon Van Gelder for an interview for *TDE*, I did not hesitate to jump at the chance. Catching up with Gordon, a two-time Hugo Award winner for Best Editor Short Form, proved to be a challenge, however, as he is taking on the duties of both editor *and* publisher of *The Magazine of Fantasy & Science Fiction*. Following is our email exchange in the fall of 2014.

The Digest Enthusiast: I've read that you didn't set out to be an editor while studying in school. To give us a little background, can you tell us about what you were studying and how the role of editor came about?

Gordon Van Gelder: I was an English major in college with a focus on creative writing, so it's not as though my studies were far afield. And in fact I edited a science fiction magazine that the science fiction club published on campus, as well as working one summer as an intern at a publishing house. I just figured all along that I'd wind up as a writer. But during my senior year, I came to realize that I didn't want to make a living as a writer. A month after graduation, I landed a job at St. Martin's Press.

TDE: What was it that told you writing as a living wasn't for you?

GVG: I realized that I don't have the right temperament for the job.

I landed a job at St. Martin's about a month after graduating from college. I was hired as an editorial assistant. I actually got the job by answering an ad in the *New York Times* (though I must note that the internship I did two years earlier helped a lot.)

TDE: After a while at *The Magazine of Fantasy & Science Fiction* (*F&SF*), you also became publisher. How do the roles of editor and publisher differ and why were you compelled to also take on the role of publisher?

GVG: To answer your second question first, I took on the role of publisher because the Fermans were looking to sell the magazine. Buy-

Albert E. Cowdrey: A Skeptical Spirit

Fantasy&ScienceFiction

DECEMBER

A Different Country
Wayne Wightman

John Langan
Eugene Mirabelli
Robert Reed
Warner Law

DISPLAY UNTIL NOV. 30

$4.50

Cover: "The Moment" by Bob Eggleton, Dec. 2008.

ing the magazine and becoming its publisher was the best way to make sure I'd be able to continue editing it.

As for how the editor and publisher roles differ, they're obviously not too far apart, since Ed Ferman and I both managed to hold down the two roles for years. As I see it, the editor's responsible for most of what goes between the covers while the publisher handles the rest. That is to say, the fiction and nonfiction are the editor's responsibility, while the publisher

Cover by Cory and Catska Ench
Sep. 2008.

handles advertising, promotion, production, and marketing.

TDE: Being on the outside looking in, it seems to me that the role of publisher would be a full time job itself! Do you ever feel that you aren't getting enough time to do one job or the other well?

GVG: I've only had that feeling, um, pretty much every day for the last 14 years. In fact, sometimes the two jobs make it hard for me to fulfill my duties as Spilogale's chief bottle-washer.

TDE: Maybe I'm missing the reference on this one— you have a pet skunk? ;-D

GVG: Chief bottle-washer just means that I handle janitorial duties around here, too.

No pet skunk, despite the company name. We do have two gerbils in the office.

TDE: As editor, are you reading story submissions straight from the submission pile? Or are you reading

examples that have already been "approved" by others? I ask this because I just read some information about *Glimmer Train* handling "40,000 submissions a year" which is something that completely blows my mind. How is that even possible? (Can you share some general numbers regarding how many submissions you're working through each year?) And can you tell us how many folks make up the *F&SF* team to get issues out on a regular basis?

GVG: When the submissions come in every day, I go through the pile and divvy them up—certain submissions go straight into my reading pile, others go to my readers, who then read through them and pass along whatever they think I should see.

In my first year, I kept track of the number of submissions and it was 20–40 a day, as I recall. (I was reading all the submissions back then.) Nowadays, I don't focus much on how many submissions we get; I worry more about their quality.

The *F&SF* team is about a dozen people, most of whom work for us on a freelance basis.

TDE: Good point about the focus now being placed on the quality. Can't argue with that at all. But do forgive me as I continue to "gosh-wow" on the numbers for a moment. With that level of submissions coming in, do you ever feel that good material is not getting a chance at publication because you have so little room to offer in each issue of *F&SF*? What are some of the difficulties you and your team face when choosing submissions?

GVG: Y'know, there are so many venues for publication now, and the barriers to publication are so low, that I don't worry about good material not getting a chance at publication.

I should note that there have been a few stories that haunted me. I published some of them in an e-book anthology called *Lonely Souls*.

The biggest difficulty we face with submissions is getting quality material of certain types and genres. We try to balance the magazine about evenly between science fiction and fantasy, but it's hard to get a good balance of first-rate material.

TDE: And after you decide that you want to run with a submission, what kinds of things happen from an editor's point of view? What are the steps that are then taken to get a submission ready for publication?

GVG: After we acquire a story, the typical process is that it goes through copyediting and then typesetting and proofreading. The authors review the manuscript in both stages, so by the time a story appears in print, it has been scoured and checked several times.

TDE: Somewhat related— what percentage of the published stories appearing in *F&SF* come from submissions? Asked a different way, do you ever "request" work from an author?

GVG: The vast majority of stories we publish—probably more than 90% of them—come from over-the-transom submissions. I'll commission stories occasionally, usually for a theme or to go with a cover illustration, but I find that over-the-transom submissions provide for us pretty reliably.

TDE: What about cover art? How does it come together?

GVG: Most of it is commissioned. I'll often get a sense

Cover by Vaughn Bode Jan. 1971.

from a story that it will suit one artist or another well and I usually trust those instincts.

TDE: Backing up a little, I've got to believe you were a voracious reader as a kid. Were you buying digests off the magazine rack or were you more interested in the longer format story found in books? What types of things were you reading?

GVG: Everyone in my family reads prodigiously. Both of my parents published some books for kids and there was never a shortage of reading material in the house—both fiction and nonfiction. I guess most of my early fiction reading was in book form but it wasn't like I discriminated between books and magazines.

With digests, as I recall, my older brother signed up for an early subscription to *IASFM* [*Isaac Asimov's Science Fiction Magazine*]—probably through Publishers Clearing House—sometime around '76 or '77. But I wasn't allowed to read his mag-

Cover by Jack Gaughan Feb. 1971.

azines. My recollection is that I got hooked on the digests (and on SF) when we were traveling on vacation in the summer of 1980. The Aug. 1980 *Analog* left a big mark on me, as did Don Wollheim's Year's Best anthology from that year, George Martin's Campbell Awards anthology, and an old Damon Knight anthology. I remember feeling they were part of a conversation . . . no, more like a family . . . that I wanted to be part of. I read the copyright lines in those books to see where the stories originally appeared. After that summer, I would pick up magazines, either by subscription or in nearby shops. I remember riding my bike a few miles across the New Jersey border into New York to find an early issue of *Twilight Zone* magazine—that must have been 1981.

TDE: Ha! So the older brother wouldn't allow you to handle his digests huh? I had an older brother like that! How old were you then? Was there ever a time when you

had a preference for the short story that generally appears in digests? Or was the attraction to science fiction firm for both short story and book length work? Given that you are publishing short stories today, where do you stand today on the matter?

GVG: Well, kids always need boundaries. As I recall, my brother's books were off-limits. I must have been about 11 when he got that subscription to *IASFM*.

I don't remember having a preference for short stories or for novels. I read lots of both. I still like both, though I've found that editing short fiction for so long has left me impatient with many novels. (Movies, too.)

TDE: Obviously, we are fans of the digest. How do you feel about the digest format in terms of the physical package? Given that *F&SF*, and the other long-running publications have been publishing in the format for a while now, do you ever feel trapped by it? Have you ever wanted to try a different print format? What do your readers say about it?

GVG: I guess I see the digest as being like the dollar bill—it's very durable and functional. There are other formats that are prettier and that stand out better on the racks, but they don't always hold up so well to the rigors of publishing a magazine regularly in America.

I've never felt trapped by the digest format. In fact, I've been encouraged a few times to try different formats and I've never particularly felt tempted. But I should own up here to being a words guy—I've always been more interested in which words are on the page than in how they look. And your questions about my early reading habits remind me of how much I prefer reading fiction in digest form. I'm a slow reader and the big pages of magazines like *Omni* were never as conducive for me for reading fiction.

When e-publishing really began to take off, it became clear that some readers like the digest format, some don't, but most are utilitarian on the matter—they're okay with any format as long as the fiction is good.

Incidentally, I had an experience about six months ago where I gave a copy of *F&SF* to someone and she said, "Oh, so that's what it looks like in print. I have an electronic subscription but I've never seen the physical magazine." Then she said, "I thought it was bigger." Wasn't there a common meme about expecting someone taller?

TDE: Can you elaborate on your comment about digests not always holding up so well to the rigors of publishing?

GVG: Actually, I said that other formats don't hold up so well to the rigors. But the digest form has taken its hits. Both *Reader's Digest* and *TV Guide* abandoned the digest format since I took over *F&SF*.

TDE: I understand that *TV Guide* is no longer in print and that *Reader's Digest* has had some troubles in recent years, however, it can still be found in print in the checkout line of most grocery stores here in the Charlotte area. I picked up the September 2014 issue they called "The Genius Issue" which I believe was the first "themed" issue they ever printed. Unfortunately no fiction included at all . . .

GVG: But is *Reader's Digest* still digest-sized? I thought it changed format . . . though a look

Cover by Maurizio Manzieri
July/Aug. 2014.

online suggests I'm mistaken. I haven't seen a copy in a checkout line around here in a long time.

TDE: Since e-publishing has come up, can you talk about how the digital subscription experience has been for *F&SF*? And how do the percentages fall between digital subscribers, print subscribers, and newsstand sales? What are the general trends in terms of subscription/print numbers for digests like *F&SF* over the past 5–10 years?

GVG: Electronic sales were chugging along for us at a small but steady pace until 2009 or so, when the whole industry took off. We wound up with a deal that gave Amazon what amounts to exclusive rights to an electronic edition of *F&SF*. That has worked out pretty well for us, though it must be said that you can't please everyone.

I don't want to get into specific sales percentages but I'll say that more people read

All Star Anniversary Issue!

Fantasy & ScienceFiction
OCT/NOV

Terry Bisson
Albert E. Cowdrey
Carol Emshwiller
Stephen King
M. Rickert
Geoff Ryman
Steven Utley
Michael Swanwick

Cover by Max Bertolini Oct/Nov 2008.

F&SF by way of print subscriptions than any other way.

TDE: As far as your particular print format goes, in 2009 you moved from a monthly publication to a bimonthly one. What prompted the change? And have you considered moving back to a monthly?

GVG: I'd been considering the change from monthly to bimonthly for a while, but it was a combination of the recession and a fairly severe change in postal rates that convinced me to switch to bimonthly. At this point, I'm not thinking of going back to a monthly schedule.

TDE: Preferring the digest format, of course we want to believe that options like *F&SF* will always be available. What kind of promotional/marketing strategies are you using to attract new readers?

GVG: In recent years, we've stuck mostly with tried-and-true strategies like direct-mail marketing. Word-of-mouth is also still strong (and I hope it always will be).

TDE: I heard you were a Yankees fan. I have to admit that I'm going to miss seeing Derek Jeter prowling around the shortstop area next year. Have we witnessed the last true Hero in baseball? Can the Yankees do it without him?

GVG: I'm sure baseball will still have plenty of heroes, but I don't know how many will wear the Yankee pinstripes. Major League Baseball made changes in the last decade that remove a lot of the advantages that big-market teams like the Yankees enjoyed for years. I think it's going to be a few years before they're back in contention. But I'll stick with 'em . . . I'm just old enough to remember some of those early 1970s teams (not to mention the early '90s teams) and the current team is in better shape than they were back then.

TDE: Another passion of mine involves searching out "RVG" and "Van Gelder" stamped into the deadwax of some of the best Jazz records ever produced. Any chance you are related to Rudy Van Gelder?

GVG: Growing up, I was told we're not related, but a few years ago, I spoke with a first cousin of Rudy's who said our families are related. The way I figure it, the closest we could be related is second cousins, once removed.

TDE: And finally, what's in store for *F&SF* readers in 2015?

GVG: Lots of good reading. *Fantasy and Science Fiction* is available in print at newsstands and by subscription from sfsite.com, where you can also purchase back issues from 1990–2014. Digital subscriptions are available on amazon.com

The Presidential Collection

Crime fiction by Lesann Berry

Senator Albert Commons prepared to receive his guest by making certain the household was empty. Bothered by a flutter of unaccustomed nervousness, he paced for two minutes in the hallway, centering his thoughts on the achievement at hand. He'd sent his housekeeper out for the evening, presenting her with a pair of expensive play tickets in honor of her fifteen years of dedicated service. In social circles, he was a conscientious employer, enjoying little turnover among domestic staff.

Less than an hour later his caller arrived.

The subdued rap on one of the double front doors echoed in the foyer. Albert stumbled from his position on the bottom step of the sweeping staircase, stiff from waiting immobile. He approached the entry and, as always, experienced a surge of pride in the regal twin American shields carved into the massive panels. The coat-of-arms confirming his family's participation in the Revolutionary War was mirrored on the door exteriors so the public might be equally well-informed. He'd always believed the interspersed sprays of olive branches introduced an organic element that complemented the patriotic images.

He paused for a count of five seconds, one hand on the antique brass knob while he drew on the persona he'd honed over decades in public office. The man he prepared to admit to his home both frightened and fascinated him, but he'd been forced to deal with the reticent fellow. Solomon Lennard specialized in unique acquisitions. He accomplished what no other could achieve. The proof of his prior successes lay a short distance down the hall.

Albert greeted his guest and with a flourish, directed the visitor to proceed through the downstairs library doorway. Patience required effort but he wanted to draw out this moment and savor the anticipation even though he chafed to examine his prize. When his companion did speak, the man's speech patterns were precise and the enunciation flawless. Proof, Albert decided, of a nationality originating outside American shores.

He indicated Lennard should sit in the single Windsor chair and circled around to stand beside his ornately carved desk. Despite his resolve, the words burning inside Albert's mouth escaped, "You've been successful?"

Lennard patted the side of his overcoat with deft fingers. His lips curled in a satisfied smile. "I have it right here."

The compact object he withdrew was wrapped in startling white cloth. He laid the item on the leather desktop pad with a soft thud. With smooth motions he unfolded and pulled aside four layers of fine cotton. The last flap of fabric revealed an antique pocket pistol. The gun lay exposed on a monogrammed square of linen.

Albert salivated. "Remarkable."

Lennard nodded at the whispered word but said nothing.

When Albert tore his gaze from the coveted sight to look fully at the procurer, the stoic expression remained unchanged. His eyes stole back to the familiar form of the Philadelphia Deringer and a fierce jolt of satisfaction infused his body. He felt light-headed with triumph. His goal lay within his grasp, three of the four obtained. He stroked a finger along the short barrel, touched the grip with a reverential hesitance.

"I am very impressed you achieved this task."

"I assume you find this endeavor worth such risk?"

Lennerd's eyes looked like dark holes in his long face.

"Assuredly." Albert confirmed. He bent to examine the small firearm beneath the yellow glow cast by the green glass shade of the desk lamp. He thought it a thing of beauty.

A percussion type handgun, the old piece had a caliber which ranged close to a .44 in modern terms, certainly capable of killing a man at minimal range. This particular gun had demonstrated that exact ability. The walnut grip, dimpled and cross-hatched with incised carvings, settled snugly against the palm. An intricate tracery of etched lines surrounded the stamped maker's mark on the flat top of the barrel. Rich German silver inlay banded a fierce eagle's head near the breech region and escutcheon. The front sight displayed a lovely dovetailed blade and fixed rear-sight tang. Even the lockplate and hammer were engraved with excellent foliate arabesque patterns.

It was an exquisite piece of workmanship despite the fact the detailed work was originally inexpensive, probably half of a set when purchased new. The gun reflected the artistry of a bygone era, an irony not lost on the viewers.

Senator Albert Commons had memorized every facet of information concerning this pocket pistol. He knew everything there was to know about the events of that fateful night at Ford's Theatre. Now he possessed the physical manifestation of the moment which changed the future of his country.

Without removing his greedy gaze, Albert offered more praise. "I'm vastly pleased with your results;

I should like to negotiate another commission." He touched the polished wood with a trembling digit, wondered if the fatal shot had been delivered by a sweaty finger or a hand held with cool concentration.

Lennard's voice came smooth as aged bourbon. "I am not indisposed to an offer."

The utter absence of inflection in the man's cadence unnerved Albert. The sound drew his complete attention. For a moment the shadows seemed heavier and denser around the still shape in the chair, the dark corners seethed as though an entity coalesced until the Senator thrust away the fancy. He cleared his windpipe and found to his disgust that his palms had gone slick with perspiration.

"I would like you to retrieve a final item of historical significance. The logistics are considerably challenging, more so even, than the recovery of the Lincoln derringer."

Lennard's gold signet ring winked in the dull light. "What singular object intrigues you?"

The mere thought of attaining the entire assemblage made Albert dizzy. The obsession to possess each of the firearms responsible for striking down an American president sent him forging ahead. "A Carcano rifle."

Lennard leaned back.

He was no more animated than the marble sculptures beside which the Senator had negotiated favors inside the gallery of the Rotunda.

After a silence lasting a full thirty seconds, Lennard nodded. "I understand. May I see the others?"

Pleasure ripped through Albert with a heat akin to sexual release but he cautiously considered the request, weighing the risk. His caller had demonstrated incredible acumen; why not indulge himself and share his achievements? After all, this man would acquire the crowning piece in his Presidential Collection.

Albert searched out and depressed a discreet button on the underside of his desk.

Both men turned to face the wall where a length of rosewood paneling cracked apart and slid open. Displayed inside was an elegantly arranged sequence of guns banded by a thick ebony frame. Two revolvers, a .32 caliber Iver-Johnson and a .44 caliber British Bulldog rested against a crimson velvet backdrop. Tiny titanium arms in the center of the case waited to cradle the Lincoln gun. Above was space for a rifle.

"The McKinley and the Garfield." Albert spiraled one veined hand to encompass the contents before he dragged his admiration from the exhibit to view the appreciation on Lennard's face. He jolted when he found the man still seated and the palm pistol pointing at his chest.

Lennard's lips twitched into an amused smile. "The Kennedy rifle always comes last. As you can imagine, the National Archives are a significant deterrent."

Albert swallowed hard.

The half-inch diameter of the muzzle directed at his torso took on the scale of a cannon mouth. He suppressed his momentary loss of composure and drew on pride to straighten his spine. Summoning the powerful voice that had given him an oratorical edge on the Senate floor, he voiced his fear in a demand. "What is your intent, Sir?"

The derringer barked. Smoke trickled out the breech. A burst of flame emitted from the barrel throat. The bullet tore a messy path through the fleshy skin in front of Albert's vocal organs.

"I'm the retrieval contingency." Lennard said.

He produced a padded sleeve from the interior of his coat and slipped each historic firearm carefully inside. The actions took only a minute to complete. He paused in the doorframe and surveyed the room. Nothing lay amiss, except for the Senator stretched out beside the desk and the pungent acrid odor of discharged gunpowder.

The door shut with a subdued click.

Two hours later Solomon Lennard reigned in what little patience remained. He pulled on his reserves as he faced the Senator's imperturbable legislative assistant inside the carefully appointed anteroom. The young man was difficult to rattle.

The aide adjusted the notepad at his elbow and offered another congenial smile. "I assure you, Senator Commons has never stayed at a lakeside motel in Wisconsin."

"Truly?" Solomon tossed one of the gloves on the conference table. The soft leather landed with a puff of air.

The aide's green eyes followed the movement but his curved lips never faltered.

"Savile Row hand coverings are made of the finest doeskin." He smoothed a palm over one sleeve of his navy blue jacket and met Solomon's steady gaze. "I have a set of my own, a gift from the Senator to each of his top staff after he was reconfirmed into office last year."

Solomon appreciated the unexpected display of loyalty for Albert Commons, a man whose political antics ranged from the normal accusations of catering to special lobbying interests, to the more serious house sub-committee inquiry during the most recent election cycle.

"Your commitment to the Senator's reputation is commendable but unnecessary." Solomon leaned back in his chair and crossed his legs and tugged the wool pant fabric taut above one knee as he considered his approach. "Albert Common's presence in a tawdry motel in the company of a nubile young woman of questionable maturity is no longer of practical concern. I want access to the man's private office."

The aide leveled his fixed gaze across the desk. "I cannot accommodate your request, sir, not without express approval from the man himself."

Solomon studied his companion and ignored the frustration curling in his abdomen. Unsurprised by the flat refusal, he felt a hint of curiosity about the lack of negative protestation or the demand for an explanation. A refreshing reaction, he decided.

Silence lengthened. Tension built. The ticking of the pendulum in the elegant Seth Thomas grandfather clock echoed from the corner. Neither man gave an inch.

Solomon opted for a more direct approach. "The Senator held in his possession an item which was not his own. I retrieve objects under the executive power of the highest level of government office." Solomon's right hand raised in a gesture to forestall speech. He allowed this information to be absorbed. After a pregnant moment he shifted his eyes to the clock and back to the aide. "Albert Commons is dead."

A brief display of panic crossed over the young man's features before the lines of his jaw hardened and his lips tightened into a flat line. Both tells indicated he'd clenched his teeth.

Solomon continued speaking; his gaze pinned on the man. "In approximately seven minutes the Senator's housekeeper will return from a well-deserved evening out and discover his corpse on the library floor. Not long after, his staff will receive official notification."

The aide rallied. He schooled his features into another impenetrable mask of good breeding although his hands clamped tightly together, whitening across the knuckles.

Solomon scanned the space again, contemplated the likelihood his surmise was incorrect and decided his first conclusion was still the most logical. Three steps away from the garish front doors of the old house, the visual had registered. The Senator had presented his stolen firearms as though Lennard was an appreciated visitor, a guest to be impressed.

The performance had been successful.

The Presidential Collection was dramatic. The spectacle of the quartet of guns, each responsible for killing a sitting Commander-in-Chief of the United States, was a macabre assemblage of political intrigue. The display board, lined with plush velvet and fitted with shiny brackets to hold the firearms, had been hidden behind an ornately carved cherry wood panel. The fifth set of prongs in the bottom middle had appeared to him as the space for an accessory or perhaps an inscribed plaque, a detail he hadn't connected until after he'd dispatched the Senator.

Sloppy work, in his opinion.

Lennard reasoned out the possibilities as he strode to the sedan waiting curbside. Plenty of assassination attempts had been carried out over the history of the country. The only other President shot during his tenure of office was Ronald Reagan. The .22 caliber pistol used by the gunman in that particular shooting had disappeared decades previously, a fact not known to the general public.

The Commons lineage had held political appointments for generations. They were a fixture in the Washington D.C. social scene, drawing on more than two centuries of interconnected relationships, favors, and influence. Solomon was confident he'd find the missing gun in the Senator's office space. The final object so coveted, that it had ignited a desire to amass the complete collection.

The Senatorial waiting room was resplendent with framed art and fine furnishings. The hand-rubbed wood of the writing table between the two men glowed with polish. A faint odor of lemon and malt told Solomon the housekeeping staff employed British cleaning products. That figured. In Revolutionary times, the Commons' family had probably been Tory sympathizers. Even the intricate design of the Aubusson carpet cushioning the soles of his black wingtips featured the Senator's prized crest emblazoned in the pile. The room reeked with the subtle iconography of extreme wealth.

Aristocratic posturing at its American best.

The aide cleared phlegm from his throat and stiffened his shoulders. He rose to his feet, pulling an ornate fob from his pocket. "After reflecting on your news, I believe I may know where the Senator kept the item you seek." He crossed the room and fit the key into the lock on the interior door.

Solomon followed.

The Senator's personal office space featured the same sartorial elegance as the vestibule. Solomon swiftly located and opened the mahogany panels of the hidden compartment. The Reagan handgun lay nestled in a bed of green velvet.

"Everyone knew of the Senator's interest in young women—" The aide's voice trailed off as he watched Solomon slip the gun inside another padded cloth sack.

Solomon Lennard tucked the bundle under his suit coat. "No one ever suspects an obsession with historic firearms."

The aide was young, perhaps twenty-five and his idealism was already tarnished. This town did that to people. He was probably the only son of an affluent family who'd spent a fortune to educate him at the finest law school and then bought an equally expensive appointment on Capitol Hill.

"What's your name?" Solomon canted his head and waited.

The aide's Adam's apple bobbed. "David Greene, Sir."

The Senator's untimely demise had shocked the aide but his resolve in the face of the unknown showed backbone.

Fingers wrapped around an object in his coat pocket, Solomon indulged his curiosity further. "Where do you come from, Mr. Greene?"

A tiny frown creased the skin between the aide's eyebrows. "Lincoln, Nebraska."

Solomon hesitated, then removed a card and extended his arm, handing the rectangle of cardstock to the other man. "Call me if you're interested in employment. The job market is difficult right now and I could use a protégé."

The phone buzzed. Both men ignored the muted sound.

Solomon departed.

His last view of the room showed David Greene framed next to the grandfather clock. He was staring at the phone, the white card clutched in his hand. ⬎

As an anthropologist, **Lesann Berry** divides her time between academic interests and professional research. Focused primarily on the American west, she is inspired by the geologic features of empty landscapes. The ancient art and prehistory of those settings often feature in her work. She writes about messed-up people and sinister events, saying her stories often feature paranormal or romantic elements because life is boring without spooky stuff and warm bodies. Crossing genre lines, she pens both contemporary and historical mysteries, romantic suspense, and even a little horror. For information about upcoming releases visit www.lesannberry.com

In Defense of Digests

Opinion by Rob Imes

To fans of science fiction, fantasy, horror, mystery and adventure, old-time radio drama and comic books, the Golden Age of the pulp magazine—roughly defined as the mid-1920s to the early 1950s—stands as a point-of-origin or "big bang" for their beloved genres. The demise of the pulps has been mourned for decades, their reputation having grown to legendary proportions. In comparison, the digest magazines are characterized as the successors to the pulps, though somehow of less keen interest. Their pages are smaller, their illustrations less emphasized (if they are illustrated at all), and generally lacking hero-themed titles as the pulps had. What's more, the digests are still with us and therefore they haven't been eulogized and romanticized in the way that the pulps have been.

Unlike the pulps, there cannot be any definitive era for the digests; their lifespan covers too many varied decades to confine to a particular time. A half-dozen long-running print digests continue to be published in our own obsessively digital age, which offers me hope that the format will be with us far longer than the skeptics might imagine. While digital proponents emphasize the convenience of e-zines, the digests can argue in favor of their own convenient format. Unlike most magazines, the sturdy digests fit perfectly on a shelf like a paperback book, no boxes needed to contain them. Despite today's high prices, the cost of a typical new issue is reasonable and affordable given the hours of reading enjoyment that they provide, especially compared with other forms of entertainment. Old digests can usually be acquired in secondary markets (like eBay) for far less money that it takes to obtain old pulps or old comic books. And most important of all perhaps is that the writing in the digests is usually of a higher quality than what can be found in the old pulps, despite the preference of many collectors for the latter.

To many fans, digests are simply the smaller-sized publications that

Ellery Queen's Mystery Magazine Nov. 1947, cover by George Salter.

came after the pulps in the timeline of history, of less interest due to their familiar presence. If one approaches a digest as the "modern equivalent of the pulps," however, then one is bound to be disappointed—just as if one were to judge Stephen King in comparison to an earlier horror writer like H. P. Lovecraft. The modern digest has its own character and ought to be judged on its own considerable merits rather than viewed in light of what it never was.

The Early Digests

Although the 1940s are remembered as the heyday of the pulps, and the 1950s as the decade of their decline due to the rise of the digests and paperbacks, all three forms co-existed in the 1940s as publishers experimented with new ways to appeal to readers with limited spending money. *Reader's Digest* magazine began in 1922, consisting then as now, of short articles reprinted from other periodicals.

Its title reflecting the use of the word "digest" to indicate a condensed presentation. The magazine's popularity, and the introduction of similarly compact sized magazines such as *Coronet* in 1936 and *Science Digest* in 1937, caused the reading public to associate the word "digest" with its physical size (around half as tall as a regular magazine) and not necessarily its contents. While non-fiction digest magazines had been published earlier, it was in the 1940s that the prose-fiction digests as we know them today would be born.

The American Mercury was a long-running magazine that contained non-fiction articles as well as some fiction. It had converted to digest size by 1936, and subsequently the magazine's business manager, Lawrence Spivak, became the publisher. Spivak soon began a line of digest-size fiction titles that would eventually be known as Mercury Publications (or Mercury Press). In 1939, paperback books debuted in the U.S. with Simon & Schuster's Pocket Books line, which consisted of less-expensive softcover versions of hardcover books. Spivak published his own version of this concept: monthly digest-size magazines which contained a full-length novel, usually abridged to fit the page count, under the series titles *Bestseller Mystery* and *Mercury Mystery*. They were surprisingly successful, lasting until the end of the 1950s, several years after Spivak had left the company.

Spivak introduced *Ellery Queen's Mystery Magazine* in late 1941 as a digest from the beginning. Initially *EQMM* (as it's known for short) consisted mostly of stories that were either reprints or printed in the

U.S. for the first time, along with an occasional original tale (such as those by Anthony Boucher in early issues). By 1943, the story introductions by editor Frederic Dannay (writing as "Ellery Queen") grew longer and more detailed, exhibiting a collector's interest in the history of the mystery genre. Another sign of the magazine's literary focus was the fact that there were no interior illustrations (and it would remain unillustrated until the 1990s), unlike mystery genre pulps of the time. *EQMM* was a 128-page digest during the 1940s (bumped up to 144 pages with a ten-cent price increase beginning in 1948), although during the war years the issues looked thinner than that. This was the result of using thinner paper to comply with paper rationing by the War Production Board. Beginning with the January 1944 issue the size of the magazine was also one-fourth of an inch shorter than before, until 1946 when it resumed its former height.

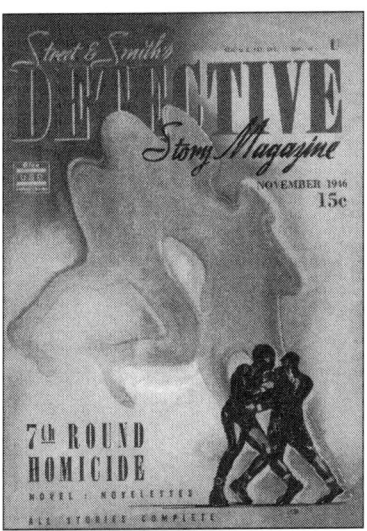

Detective Story Magazine Nov. 1946.

At the same time, pulp giant Street & Smith made similar changes to the way they published their magazines, converting their pulp line into digests. The first to make the change was the long-running (since 1915!) *Detective Story Magazine*, which debuted as a digest with the October 1943 issue. *Astounding Science Fiction* converted to digest the following month, as did the popular pulp heroes *The Shadow* (beginning with Dec. 1943) and *Doc Savage* (beginning Jan. 1944). *Unknown*, a fantasy-themed pulp edited by *Astounding*'s John W. Campbell, Jr., was scheduled to convert to digest-size with the Dec. 1943 issue, but the series was cancelled due to low circulation. Publishers had a limited amount of paper to use during wartime, and the conversion to the digest format may have been borne more out of necessity than any aesthetic preference.

The digest form, however, had the effect of distancing these former pulps from their previous format's poor reputation. Just as *EQMM* was more respectable and literary-minded than most mystery magazines, Street & Smith's digest line, with its now sedate covers, separated themselves from their lurid pulp counterparts. This was particularly true for *Astounding* which was already known among serious science fiction fans as being more adult-oriented than its pulp competitors such as Raymond A. Palmer's *Amazing Stories*. When one of the first-ever SF anthologies was published in 1946 (*Adventures in Time and Space*, edited by Raymond J. Healy and J. Francis McComas) the majority of stories within were from the pages of *Astounding*. Each issue of *Astounding* also contained at

The Magazine of Fantasy #1 Fall 1949.

least one "science fact" article, with pages sometimes printed on slick paper for better reproduction of the photographs that accompanied it. This serious style, in addition to its small size, helped distinguish *Astounding* from the competition.

EQMM had a fantasy-themed companion magazine beginning in 1949 when *The Magazine of Fantasy* debuted, published by Mercury Press and edited by Anthony Boucher and J. Francis McComas. With its second issue, the title was changed to *The Magazine of Fantasy and Science Fiction* (or *F&SF* for short) and like *EQMM* and *Astounding/Analog*, this notable digest magazine continues to this day. *F&SF*'s focus was on the literary quality of the fiction and less on either the science or pulpy trappings, effectively carving a place for itself apart from every other magazine on the stands. Like *EQMM*, there were no interior illustrations, aside from an occasional *New Yorker*-style cartoon or a page

reserved for Gahan Wilson, which reinforced its image as being for the more sophisticated SF reader.

The drawback to an overly mature approach to a genre like science fiction is when it makes the subject matter look dull, and the popularity of *Astounding* began to decline in the 1950s when it was no longer the primary source for quality SF. Its main challenger was *Galaxy Science Fiction* which debuted in 1950. *Galaxy* was able to walk the line between the literary and escapist tastes of its readers to become one of the most influential SF magazines of the 1950s and 1960s, its fame further spread through anthology collections that bore the magazine's name (*The Third Galaxy Reader*, etc.). There were also "Galaxy novels," full-length novels published in the digest magazine format rather than as paperback books. The look of *Galaxy*'s covers, with their white borders, was imitated by the short-lived EC science fiction comics, as well as other digests such as *Space Science Fiction* (which usually had a yellow border). *Galaxy* stories were adapted for radio on the series *X Minus One*—replacing the show's previous source of stories, *Astounding*.

In the sixth issue (March 1951), editor H. L. Gold reported on the feedback from readers on its debut: "The physical makeup of *Galaxy* has been overwhelmingly approved, less than 10% arguing for either large or pulp format. The large size, 8½" x 11", allows better display, but at the expense of portability. The pulp format is a relic of the 1920s and should properly be displayed alongside illuminated manuscripts." (My friend Dwight Decker points out that "the two SF magazines of the

1920s, *Amazing* and *Wonder Stories*, were bedsheet size, not pulp-size!" Bedsheet size is around 9" x 12".) Of course it could be said that the main asset of *Galaxy* was the quality of the work appearing in its pages, and not the size of the pages themselves.

Famous Fantastic Mysteries May 1951.

Digests vs. Pulps

Numerous SF digests began appearing in the 1950s after the success of *Galaxy* and *F&SF*, however most of them died before the decade was over. An exception was *Galaxy*'s companion magazine, *If*, as well as Ziff-Davis' *Amazing* (converting from pulp to digest in 1953) and *Fantastic* (which debuted in 1952 as an attempt at a prestige digest, until its standards slipped). The success of the digest *Fantastic* caused readers in Ziff-Davis' pulp *Fantastic Adventures* to wonder (in the letter pages) when *FA* would fold as a result. The two *Fantastic*s co-existed until March 1953 when the pulp ended, merging with the digest. The digest ran until 1980 when it merged with its sister magazine, *Amazing*.

Pulps continued to be published in the 1950s, but changes began to be made in their formats. Traditionally pulps had ragged, untrimmed edges unlike digests' smooth, square edges. In 1953, *Startling Stories* was reduced by an inch, with trimmed edges, but remained pulp size (6¾" x 9"). *Future Science Fiction* made the same change in 1953, but eventually converted to digest size (the magazine folded in 1960). One of the most famous pulps, the long-running *Weird Tales*, converted from pulp to digest size after July 1953. The next issue, the editor noted, "will be the first in our small handy size; it will be easier to read, con-

venient to carry and—as always in the past—full of the best in fantasy fiction." Seven issues of the digest-size *Weird Tales* were published until giving up the ghost in late 1954.

Not all pulps converted to digest—some converted back to pulp. In 1951, the long-running pulp *Famous Fantastic Mysteries* published a few issues in an appealing format that was slightly larger than the usual digest size. It measured 6¼" x 8½" (a half-inch wider than Dell/Penny Press' current digests) and had trimmed edges, but apparently was not embraced by all of *FFM*'s readers and the untrimmed pulp format returned after a few issues. In the letters page of the October 1951 issue (where it had converted back to untrimmed pulp format), one reader wrote "the old [pulp-size] *FFM* had a breath of the good old days about it. . .Why don't I enjoy it [the digest-size] as much as formerly? Just nostalgia, I guess."

Another reader was more vehement. In the May 1951 (digest) issue,

TO BE MORE READABLE, more compact, more apparent—next issue WEIRD TALES is making its first important change in format in thirty years, and going to digest size. In your pocket you will be able to carry ghosts and goblins, werewolves and vampires, witches and spells. . . . Our stories will be just as good, our authors headliners as in the past, but we shall be all solid reading matter (no advertising), printed on better paper and more convenient to carry and to read.

SO BEGINNING WITH THE NEXT NUMBER —OUT JULY 1st—WATCH FOR YOUR FAVORITE FANTASY MAGAZINE IN ITS NEW SIZE . . . .

ALWAYS THE BEST

Weird Tales' digest announcement from the July 1953 issue.

a reader wrote: "Over the past few years there has been a tendency for some publishers to bring out their magazines in a digest-sized form, and this has been encouraged by a small, but vocal, group of snobbish fans who sneer at any 'pulp' magazine, and hail as 'adult' anything appearing in digest size. In my opinion, these fans are suffering from an inferiority complex—they want to show their fantasy magazines to their friends, but are ashamed of those which are conventional pulp size. I was prepared for all the new publishers in the field to pander to this minority group by restricting their magazines to digest size, but I never expected Popular Publications to slavishly follow this current trend. In my opinion, it is a fad which will not last long."

The narrative of the digest magazines supplanting the pulps is a familiar one, but it's a simplification considering that the two formats co-existed for several years. The digests "replaced" the pulps only in the sense that the digests survived while the pulps did not. Of the five prose-fiction digests still published today, only one of them (*Analog*) began as a pulp (as *Astounding*), and its conversion to digest form was in 1943, a decade before the demise of the pulps. The digests have their own unique history, parallel and subsequent to the pulps, with their own distinctive character from the beginning. For that reason it's misleading to think of them as modern versions of the pulps, a format that many of them never were, and never tried to be like.

A digest-size issue of *The Shadow* Mar. 1945.

Other Worlds #21 Aug. 1952.

Some pulps became digests, but there were also a few digests that became pulps. During the mid-1940s, the famous pulps *The Shadow* and *Doc Savage* were published in the digest format, only to end their long runs in the larger pulp size in 1949. Ray Palmer's *Other Worlds* began as a digest in 1949 but by 1955 had converted to the larger pulp size. *Fantastic Universe* began as a digest in 1953, until the end of its run in 1959–60 when it converted to full-size. Publishers continued to experiment with formats for decades to come, while the last of the traditional ragged-edge pulps either converted to a new model or died out.

The first issue of the long-running *Alfred Hitchcock's Mystery Magazine* (or *AHMM* for short) appeared in December 1956, as a result of the popularity of the TV series *Alfred Hitchcock Presents* which had debuted the year before. From the beginning, *AHMM* was a digest, but briefly in 1957, the magazine went full-size (8¼" x 11") albeit with a reduced page count, thereby maintaining its 35 cents cover price. Despite the increased visibility that a larger size might attract, the simple illustrations within didn't really deserve to be seen bigger and took up more space than they would have in the smaller size.

In the final issue of the full-size experiment (Jan. 1958), the editor (who always wrote as "Alfred Hitchcock") explained that bowing to reader wishes, subsequent issues would be "in the pocket or digest size" and noted the smaller format's benefits: "Letters have continually urged me to make this change. Women confided they are able to maneuver a smaller sized magazine into their bag. (Should this be encouraged?) Both men and women claimed the small size is handier. (Our civilization is indeed making softies of us.) Students boasted they could read a petite magazine more easily during study

Alfred Hitchcock's Mystery Magazine #1 Dec. 1956.

Forgotten Fantasy #1 Oct. 1970.

periods, fitting it neatly behind a facade of textbook. (Boys will be boys, and discerning ones.)" *AHMM* has remained a digest to this day.

Analog (as *Astounding* was retitled in 1960) also converted into a full-size publication from March 1963 to March 1965, to resemble the other slick, full-size magazines of publisher Condé Nast (who had replaced Street & Smith as the publisher a few years earlier) and to provide more page space for high-paying advertisers. As with *AHMM*'s attempt, the page count was halved in order that the cover price would remain unchanged. While the science fact articles benefited from the larger size, having more space for photographs on the page, and the amount of full-page advertisements increased, the fiction and their illustrations were not necessarily helped by the change. Although artists with detailed styles like Virgil Finlay could still be found drawing for the digest magazines, most

illustrations in digests of the 1960s tended to be simpler, more suited for the smaller size. (Finlay passed away in 1971, the same year that *Analog* editor John W. Campbell died.)

The late 1960s and early 1970s saw a resurgence of interest in the pulps and many of the old stories (reprinted exactly from their original appearances, including illustrations) appeared in numerous reprint digest magazines, especially from Ultimate Publishing, home to *Amazing* and *Fantastic*. These reprints make a nice alternative for anyone who wishes to read the old pulps without getting wood chips all over themselves. Pulps also found renewed life in the 1960s–80s as paperback books, then later as larger trade paperback-size replica editions. Famous pulps such as *Weird Tales* and *Black Mask* were revived more than once in these new formats, and heroes like The Shadow, Doc Savage, The Spider and Conan have continually been reprinted in book form.

Forgotten Fantasy was a short-lived all-reprint digest magazine that lasted only five issues (Oct. 1970 to June 1971). It was inspired by the legacy of *Famous Fantastic Mysteries* in offering obscure and hard-to-find fantasy classics. In the letters page of the final issue (which was not planned to be the last), a reader objected to the "absurdly small size" and predicted a possible revival of the pulp format due to another fantasy digest, *Coven 13*, having recently moved to full-size under a new title, *Witchcraft & Sorcery*. The editor replied: "I, too, mourn the passing of the pulp magazine, but I don't believe it will ever return. It belongs to our past, like the Saturday

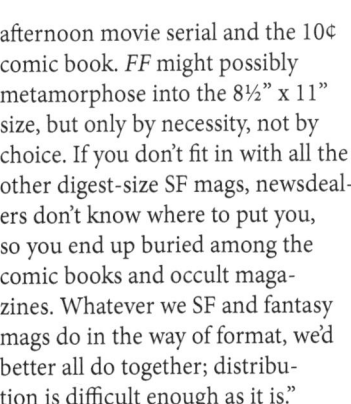

Coven 13 #1 Sep. 1969, with cover artwork by William Stout.

The first publication of "Enders Game" *Analog* Aug. 1977.

afternoon movie serial and the 10¢ comic book. *FF* might possibly metamorphose into the 8½" x 11" size, but only by necessity, not by choice. If you don't fit in with all the other digest-size SF mags, newsdealers don't know where to put you, so you end up buried among the comic books and occult magazines. Whatever we SF and fantasy mags do in the way of format, we'd better all do together; distribution is difficult enough as it is."

Digests vs. Slicks

In an article title "The End of the Ghetto?" (*Galileo* #5, Oct. 1977), Alexei and Cory Panshin wrote: "In the Thirties, sf magazines took on the appearance of the racy pulp story magazines of the day, a publishing form that died with the advent of television and the paperback book. Since the late Fifties, magazine fiction of all kinds has become rare, the emphasis of sf

publishing has clearly shifted to the pb [paperback book], and the few remaining sf magazines have been digest-sized pulps, remnants from another period, fossils confined to a tuckaway corner of the newsstand. New readers of science fiction, like students of ours at Cornell a few years ago, could feel that *Galaxy* and *Analog* and *Fantastic* and the like may safely be ignored, secure in the knowledge that anything in them worth the bother of reading would show up pretty soon as a paperback novel or in an anthology."

One advantage of following the magazines, however, is to discover stories first, before others have decided what is worth reprinting later. A few months before the Panshins' article was published, the August 1977 issue of *Analog* hit the stands, containing a new novelette titled "Ender's Game" by Orson Scott Card. The Panshins' students would have had to wait until March 1980

Omni Dec. 1978.

for its first reprinting in paperback form. (In terms of waiting time, this would be like not bothering to see *Star Wars* until *The Empire Strikes Back* came out.) "Ender's Game" was expanded and published as a novel in 1985, and adapted as a motion picture in 2013. Many stories that originally appeared in digest magazines have provided the content for subsequent paperback books and movies. Rather than being seen as an avoidable, extraneous step for a story to enter public awareness, the magazines ought to be regarded as a vital outlet through which material of future significance may be born. (Some worthwhile magazine fiction, of course, is never reprinted, waiting to be rediscovered.)

Just as H. L. Gold had earlier compared pulps to ancient documents, to favor the new digest format, the Panshins used disparaging language ("fossils," etc.) to describe digests in the 1970s. In their article, the Panshins noted that four new sf magazines had debuted in the past year: "*Galileo, Cosmos, Unearth,*

and *Isaac Asimov's Science Fiction Magazine.* Only the last of these has been cast in the old familiar, digest-sized, scaled-down pulp format we are used to. The other magazines have been experiments, attempts to present sf magazines in new and contemporary form." And yet, of those four new magazines, it was only that "scaled-down pulp" called *Asimov's* which is still with us today. The other three were gone by 1981. Could it be that *Asimov's* digest format is a still-new and still-contemporary form after all?

The Panshins envisioned the creation of a slick, million-reader circulation magazine with high production values, "with graphics as advanced as those to be found on contemporary record jackets, with money to pay two or five times the rates of *Analog*." Such a magazine appeared exactly one year later with the debut of *Omni* magazine. It had the slick production values of *Playboy* along with (in its debut issue) stories by Asimov, Theodore Sturgeon and Ron Goulart in addition to fact-based articles. *Omni's* fiction editor in its first few years was Ben Bova, former editor of *Analog*. How did this magazine-of-the-future fare compared to those "fossil" digests? *Analog* and *Asimov's* are still with us, but *Omni* ceased publication in 1995.

It would be a mistake, however, to draw lessons from this history—for example to conclude that a slick, full-size magazine represents a failed past since the digests endure. There were digests that also failed during that time period. While *Asimov's* was thriving by 1980, both *Galaxy* and *Fantastic* folded. A magazine's format has never been a guarantee of its success or survival. A large-size companion publication to *Asimov's*, titled *Asimov's SF Adventure Magazine*, had appeared in 1978, but was cancelled after four issues. In the 1990s, both *Amazing Stories* and *Fate* magazine switched from digest to slick full-size magazines—and eventually back again. One format doesn't necessarily represent the past, the other the future. I believe this holds true as well for digital formats compared to print, despite the prevalence of the notion today that digital is the future, print the past. Both *Omni* and *Galaxy* attempted to continue their existence in digital form early on, after the demise of their print incarnations, and both failed. The current web-based *Amazing Stories* is so different in style and purpose from the previous magazine versions that any comparison between them is apples and oranges.

Even the digest magazines themselves have not remained uniform in their dimensions, occasionally reducing or increasing size due to printer changes or cost-cutting. In the December 2008 issue of *Asimov's*, editor Sheila Williams gave an overview of the magazine's adjustments in size over the years. "When *Asimov's* was founded in 1976," she wrote, "the fiction digest size had been standardized at five-and-one-eighth by seven-and-five-eights. *Asimov's* size was reduced slightly in 1984 and again in 1989 to save on production costs. The second size adjustment meant that our publisher's four fiction digests were now exactly the same size as the *TV Guide* and could be produced at the same printer during *TV Guide*'s down time. In June 1998, we moved to a new printer, and the

The first issue of the full-size *Asimov's SF Adventure Magazine* Fall 1978.

magazines increased to a non-digest format called an 'F-trim size.' Our production circumstances recently changed once again, which is why your new issue of *Asimov's* is what's known in the trade as an 'L-trim size' magazine. We have fewer pages now, too, but, because the leaves are larger, we're only a handful of pages shorter than we were previously."

The October 2008 issue of *Locus* reported on the change, quoting Williams' explanation to the readers. "The reason for the change is nothing to be alarmed by," she wrote. "Paper and production costs have presented *Asimov's* and our sister publication, *Analog*, with a choice: increase subscription rates and single-issue costs to retain the old format, or adopt a slightly different size and retain our current prices. Naturally, we felt it was of best benefit to all to choose the latter." *Locus* noted that the new size conforms to that of Dell/Penny Press' puzzle and astrology publications, but warned

Alfred Hitchcock Mystery Magazine
Dec. 2014, with a Todd Davidson cover.

that "others are less sanguine about the format change, worrying it could be the death knell for these magazines, as readers might find it harder to locate them on the newsstands." (They didn't explain why they thought a larger size would be harder to find.) Although Williams refers to the new size as a "non-digest format," the slightly larger size of the current issues are still considered by most readers to be digests, given that they remain smaller than a regular full-size magazine, and smaller than even the shrunken pulps of the mid-1950s such as *Startling Stories* and *Science Fiction Quarterly*.

Looking Ahead

It is said that history is written by the winners, but the lack of recognition that is often given toward digests suggests that their history has been written by those who favored the losers, the pulp magazines that had died out. The value of the digest magazines has been eclipsed by nostalgia for those who came before them, for those who didn't survive. Hopefully it won't require the demise of the digests for their own worth to be recognized.

The future is defined by what still exists today to affect tomorrow, and as long as the digest magazines continue to be published, and continue to be bought and read and enjoyed, then they are by definition new and contemporary despite the age of their particular publishing model. It would be just as unfair to compare the internet to a "fossil" due to the prevalence of "dead links." As long as there are those who still provide content for that format, and readers willing to purchase it, the digest magazine should continue well into the future. For those like myself who prefer that format, our responsibility is to support them and spread the word about them— not take them for granted, figuring that they'll always be around. In truth, the digest magazines need no "defense"; their continued survival is its own self-evident proof of their value among readers. ⅃

Rob Imes is the editor and publisher of *Ditkomania*, a zine devoted to the work of Steve Ditko. Single issues are $3.00 postpaid. A 4-issue subscription is $12.00 postpaid. (Inquire for destinations outside the United States.)

Rob Imes
13510 Cambridge #307
Southgate, MI 48195

Visit the Ditkomania page on Facebook.

Rob is also the chairman of the United Fanzine Organization (UFO) and publisher of their club zine, *Tetragrammaton Fragments*. You can download a free pdf of *T-Frags* from their website
unitedfanzineorganization.weebly.com

Fate Magazine Trading Cards
Article by Rudolph Schmidt

In 1996, *Fate* magazine began a series of 51 collector's trading cards. They may have been created as a marketing promotion by *Fate*'s publisher at that time, Llewellyn Worldwide. Whatever their genesis, they make a wonderful collectible.

The cards are printed on heavy weight card stock in nine, 8.5" x 11" sheets (or sets) with perforated borders separating the cards. The front of each card features a different cover from *Fate*'s colorful history, with glossy finish. The selections span the years from 1948 to 1998, thankfully bypassing the profusion of lackluster text-only covers.

The uncoated card backs list the stats: date, year, volume and issue, whole number issue, a description of the lead story, and the card number. Set one through five, and set nine, include six cards each. Set six through eight include five cards each.

It seems counterintuitive, but the copyright dates on the sets raise a question as to whether they were issued in numerical order. Sets one through four, and set six are © 1996, set five, seven and eight are © 1997, and set nine is © 1998.

Although described as a limited-edition set, you can still purchase them new, directly from *Fate* magazine for $9.95 plus shipping and handling. Mine were sent in a vinyl sleeve and included a cover letter signed by Editor-in-Chief, Phyllis Galde.

The introduction on set one states: "For nearly 50 years FATE magazine has enlightened and entertained its readers with true reports of the strange and the unknown." A true statement in 1996. Since then, the copy has been updated by hand, with "50" overwritten by "60," in pen. An unfortunate blemish to an otherwise pristine set of cards.

Most of the items in the *Fate* online shop are various subscriptions and back issues, but in addition to the trading cards, an extensive series of 11" x 17" cover posters are also available for $11.95 each. ⚡

The Big Story
Article by Charlie Jacobs

A true crime story was the catalyst for a radio, television and digest series. The introduction from *The Big Story* #1 explains. Producer Barnard J. Prockter, "read that the Simga Delta Chi [journalism] award had been given to James McGuire of the *Chicago Times* for his investigations clearing Joseph Majczck of a 99-year murder sentence. Prockter saw in that case a model for his program."

The Big Story began as an NBC radio program on April 2, 1947. It dramatized true crime stories straight from the front pages of America's newspapers, purportedly solved through the tenacity of reporters who refused to give up after the local police had moved on. The program, which ran until March 23, 1955, was a hit, rivaling competition from Bing Crosby's *Philco Radio Time* on ABC (1946–1949). *The Big Story* was developed by producer Barnard J. Prockter and writer Clement Wyle. Writers included Gail Ingram, Arnold Pearl and Max Ehrlich. The theme for both the radio, and later television program,

came from Richard Strauss' tone poem, *Ein Heldenleben* (A Hero's Life). The radio series was directed by Tom Victor and Harry Ingram.

Co-creator Wyle who kept archives for Lewis E. Lawes, Warden of Sing Sing (1920–1941), collected a storehouse of true crime stories. In addition, Prockter and Wyle interviewed hundreds of reporters to find dramatic stories to recreate on the air. Their selections required the reporter to have been an integral part of the investigation. Unlike most popular fiction today, *The Big Story* journalists and local police often worked together, with the reporter following up on leads that nearly always helped solve the case.

Over its run, the program brought a moment of national recognition to dozens of dedicated reporters; including a few already famous like Walter Winchell, Dorothy Kilgallen and Dan Parker.

As each episode drew to a close, announcer Ernest Chappell, read a telegram with final comments about the featured case from its real life reporter, and awarded the journalist a $500 prize on behalf of the sponsor, Pall Mall (which changed to Lucky Strike during the radio program's final two years). Actors dramatizing the stories included Ralph Bell, Robert Dryden, Alice Frost, Betty Garde, Arnold Moss, Mercedes McCambridge, Santos Ortega, and many others.

The program was narrated by Bob Sloane, who also hosted the television adaptation of the series which debuted on September 16, 1949. Other hosts during its eight seasons on TV were Norman Rose, Ben Grauer and Burgess Meredith. The half-hour program finished its run on NBC on June 28, 1957, but continued in syndication with its final season ending in 1958. The series was nominated for a Primetime Emmy Award in 1953. In 2012, GAC Video Classics released a DVD collection of 14 episodes on two disks from the 1957–58 season, hosted by Meredith.

The television edition of the program provided work for dozens and dozens of actors including James Broderick, Ross Martin, Jack Warden, Maxine Stuart, Richard Carlyle, James Gregory, James Dean, Jason Robards, Jean Alexander, Louis Gossett Jr., Leslie Nielsen, Lois Nettleton, Anthony Perkins, Sam Jaffe, Joyce Van Patten, Diane Ladd, Walter Matthau, Warren Oats and Jerry Stiller.

In 1951, Markrite Enterprises published three issues of *The Big Story* digest, based on "America's Radio and Television Favorite." The monthly magazine appeared on newsstands in issues dated October, November and December, and then disappeared.

The Big Story on DVD.

Each issue featured "authentic stories as they actually happened, faithfully reported by the men and women of the press." Under the editorial direction of Walter B. Gibson, author of *The Shadow, Psychic Sciences* and many, many other books and novels, *The Big Story* featured six true crime stories in every edition.

All three covers sported full color paintings by Avrom Winfield, printed on glossy paper stock. Interior pages were printed on a stock slightly better than the standard newsprint common to digests—just enough to provide a better printing surface for the numerous black-and-white photographs that illustrated the stories.

It's a minor detail, but contents pages in *The Big Story* were oddities. Each one lists the issue's contents out of order. The page numbers are included so readers can locate what's coming up next, but the order of each issue's six cases seem to be random. One can't help wonder what Art Director, Jesse Jacobs

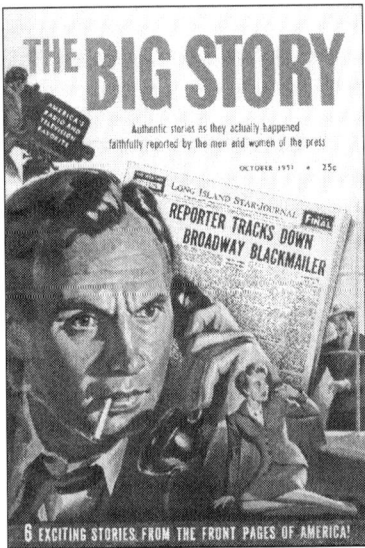

The Big Story #1 Oct. 1951.

had in mind with this approach.

All of the names of the people involved in *The Big Story*'s cases were changed, with the exception of the real life reporter. Numerous photographs re-enact the actual events with models dramatizing the action—hence the need for the Director of Photography, Andre De Rona. At least one actor/model, Owen Jorden, also appeared in the teleplay portraying Andrew Viglietta, of the *Long Island Star Journal*.

The names of the reporters and their newspapers are listed on the contents page and in story sidebars, but the stories themselves are uncredited. They're all written in third person, rather than first, which leads me to believe they were not written by the reporters themselves. Perhaps they were the work of Managing Editor Bernard M. Skolsky and/or Contributing Editor Edwin V. Burkholder, but we'll probably never know.

The first issue got off to a strong start. Six fascinating and varied cases

that entailed: clearing a man arrested for murder, convicting a black widower, solving the murder of an 18-year-old girl, tracking down a serial killer, outwitting a sociopathic extortionist, and rectifying a case of mistaken identity. Each story places the reporter in the center of the action, sharing information with local police, sometimes in partnership and others as a reluctant outsider.

As presented, the tenacity of the reporters is a common thread in their success in uncovering the truth. It's summed up in the debut issue in "The Strange Case of the Murderer's Double." "Some of the greatest stories of all time, [Julian] Houseman knew, had been gained by reporters who stayed with them. Often some false lead would be accepted by the press at large, leaving opportunity for a keen reporter to score a scoop. Here was a story with a ninety-nine and nine-tenths average against it, but the one shot in a thousand would be a sensation if it came through."

During the digest's short run, only two women were among the 18 featured journalists. In both cases they put themselves in harm's way to get the story. In issue #1, when Margrete Daney fills in for a colleague at the *Toledo Blade* she quickly finds herself the lead reporter on the city's infamous serial killer case as "The Mad Clubber Strikes Again."

Daney's first front page story struck home personally. The victim of the clubber's second attack survived, but the third did not. A librarian, who years earlier had introduced a young girl to the wonderful world of books and encouraged her to write. A young girl who grew up to become the reporter covering her mentor's murder.

Even with the city on high alert and increased police surveillance, a week later, another victim, a young nurse on her way to check on a patient, increased the number of murders to three. Again, Daney knew the victim. They had attended high school together.

Daney's editor, Martin Dennis, cautions the reporter to remain objective and not get emotionally involved in the story. But Daney is unable to distance herself. The more she thinks about the murdered women, the more she wants to do something about it.

When a fourth body is found, a high school girl, Daney can stand it no longer. Against her editor's better judgement, she coerces him into standing by while she poses as bait for the clubber. She camouflages a World War II helmet with flowers and velvet. After dark she strolls nervously through the area where the clubber had claimed his first victim.

"Then it happened, with such terrifying suddenness that Margrete never fully remembered what did take place. Out of the darkness came a lunging form. She saw the club over her head. She ducked. The club came down, grazing her side. She let out a scream that could be heard for blocks and then everything went black."

After Daney's scream, Dennis rushes to her aid, as the clubber flees. Unfortunately, neither get a good look at him. The police are not happy with Daney's interference in their investigation. Apparently spooked, the clubber is silent for eight weeks following Daney's botched attempt to trap him.

But eventually, he strikes again. This time his victim is an eleven-year-old girl, beaten while her father was away from their home visiting his wife in the hospital. Police conclude the killer must be someone who lives in the neighborhood and knew of the family's whereabouts. They round up potential suspects from the area and bring them in for questioning.

Earlier, Daney had gone to the morgue to see the body. There, she noticed an unusual mark on the girl's cheek. At the line-up she spots a ring worn by one of the suspects. A ring, she suggests to the detective in charge, that may have left a mark like the one on the victim's face. The man is detained while the crime lab examines his ring. They soon find traces of blood.

A lengthy interrogation follows and eventually the man confesses. At his trial, his identity as the mad clubber is confirmed and Margrete Daney at last concludes her Big Story.

In issue #3 we learn about "The Downfall of Annie the Pig," in which a determined twenty-year-old female reporter named Kathryn Steffan goes undercover at a notorious

> "Then it happened, with such terrifying suddenness that Margrete never fully remembered what did take place. Out of the darkness came a lunging form. She saw the club over her head."

The Big Story #2 Nov. 1951.

Women's Prison to expose the brutality of its matron. After her arrival, tension builds as Steffan and another prisoner are thrown into the "sweat box" for defending another inmate.

"The room was small, hardly big enough for Betty and Kathryn as they stood in the darkness. There was no window, no light to penetrate the Stygian blackness. At their heads was a hole that lead to the furnace room and the hot air from there poured into the darkness, smothering the two with a sickening and stupefying heat."

The women's situation degenerates further, with Steffan fearing for her life until a last minute rescue by her colleagues at the newspaper and the police. The matron is arrested and charged with assault.

After a series of articles about the County Farm: "An aroused and angry public demanded a quick and thorough clean up. Some months later Kathryn was back in the Bastille, but it was hard to recognize the place. Windows had been placed in the thick walls and sunshine came inside. The girls had individual cells, which were neat and clean. There were class-rooms where they were given instruction during their detention period. The dining room was homey and immaculate, and the food as good and as appetizing as found in almost any home."

The quality of the writing, or perhaps editing, seemed rushed in the final edition. In one particularly disruptive example from "The Blubbering Boy Bandits" (December 1951), Lieutenant Ray Jennings addresses reporter Eddie Griffin. "Finding this car was a break; from the way it's cluttered with cigarette butts, a couple of kids must have used it. Old hands wouldn't have left such clues. No marks of lipstick though, so the girl angle is out."

"So the girl angle was out."

A simple mistake, but one that jars the reader out of the narrative flow. Perhaps it was an early hint the magazine was dead on arrival. Nevertheless, the radio and television programs each enjoyed several more years on the air.

How accurate were *The Big Story*'s dramatizations? How important a role did the reporters actually play in solving the crimes? Of course it varied, but Richard W. O'Donnell, in the *Nostalgia Digest*, revealed his friend, the late Leonard Lerner, of the *Boston Globe*, was the featured reporter on the June 1, 1956 episode of the TV program. Lerner confided he did not confront the gunman or convince him to surrender as dramatized. "All I had to do was call the police, and tell them where he was hiding."

The Big Story #2 leads with

"Death Scores a Bull's Eye," featuring James Fusco of *The Columbus Citizen*. The murder case, involving an Ohio State University student and professor, made national news. Dates never appear in the digest, but its cases are written to appear as if contemporary. Without some research, a reader might never suspect this one was from 1929, a twenty-two year old story by 1951.

> "Realizing then that her skull was fractured and to relieve her suffering, I severed her jugular with my pocket knife."

In 2010, two books were written about the case, *The Professor and the Coed: Scandal and Murder at the Ohio State University* by Mark Gribben and *Gold Medal Killer: The Shocking True Story of the Ohio State Professor—an Olympic Champion—and his Coed Lover* by Diana Britt Franklin.

Of course all of the names were changed, but what follows are comparisons between the digest's fictionalization and the facts as reported in Gribben's account.

Drama: Victim Jean Toomer described as "pretty as a picture."

Fact: Victim Theora Hix described as "moderately attractive."

Drama: Cause of death, "a small, heavily leaded blackjack" to knock her unconscious, followed by "a surgeon's scalpel . . . severing the carotid artery, a delicate and difficult job for any surgeon."

Fact: Cause of death, "hammer blows" "her face was battered almost beyond recognition," a "gapping cut that ran across her throat nearly from ear to ear"

and "stab wounds were visible on her back and abdomen."

Drama: During a police interview, Professor Alfred Bayne says he returned his landlord's keys the day he read of Toomer's murder. Reporter James Fusco cracks the case when he produces a newspaper clipping from the day in question. The victim had not been identified at that point. Only the murderer would have known her identity.

Fact: Dr. James Howard Snooks was interrogated in a sixteen-hour grilling and slapped by Franklin County prosecutor John Chester Jr. hard enough to leave red marks on his cheeks. Exhausted and disoriented, he eventually signed a confession which he claimed at his trial had been written by Chester. Below is an excerpt:

"...she remonstrated with me against leaving the city with my family for the week-end as I had previously planned to do.

"She threatened that if I did go that she would take the life of my wife and baby. During the quarrel she grabbed for the purse in which she sometimes kept a .41-caliber Derringer which I had given her.

"In the struggle she was hit on the head with a hammer with the intent to stun her. She continued desperately and an increased number of blows of increasing force was necessary to stop her. Realizing then that her skull was fractured and to relieve her suffering, I severed her jugular with my pocket knife."

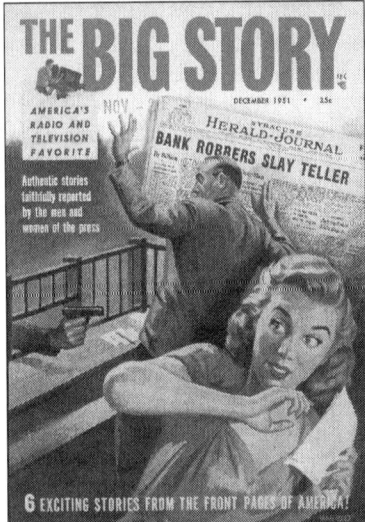

The Big Story #3 Dec. 1951.

but kept the major events and outcomes intact. As writer and journalist John Hersey once wrote, "Journalism allows its readers to witness history; fiction gives its readers an opportunity to live it."

The Big Story put its audience in the middle of each story. It used its platform to entertain, sell cigarettes and present a world with greater order and justice than the one we live in. Its underlying themes were that crime will always be punished and that justice will always prevail if you work hard and long enough to uncover the facts. Like fiction, it presented a simpler, idealized version of reality.

As true crime magazines go, *The Big Story* was one of the best. Despite its flaws, its stories were less sensational, less graphic and probably more accurate than its competition. It's unfortunate the magazine was short lived. It's easy to find copies of the radio program online—and if you work hard and long enough you can uncover DVDs of the TV show and copies of the original digest. ⚡

During the trial, newspaper coverage continued daily with caricaturists, among them, Milton Caniff, depicting key moments and portraits of jurors. A case can be made that his work on the Snooks trial contributed to Caniff's rising success, which led him to New York City, where he created the *Terry and the Pirates* comic strip in 1934.

The Big Story presented each reporter's role as an integral part of each investigation, with savvy observations and tenacity unmatched by local authorities. Grippen's book presents a significantly different version of the reporter's work in the Snooks-Hix investigation. Initially, the *Columbus Citizen* reported a group of scientists from Washington DC felt the murder was due to "the blind and absolutely uncontrolled, even unconscious, rage of the epileptic."

The fictionalized version rewrote or invented many of the details and some of the supporting evidence,

References

• *Nostalgia Digest* Winter 2004: "The Big Story" by Richard O'Donnell
• "Newspaper Heroes on the Air: The Big Story" by Bob Stepno
http://jheroes.com/Jerry Haendiges Vintage
• Radio Logs episode list:
http://www.otrsite.com/logs/logb1047.htm
• *Broadcasting Telecasting* July 3, 1950
http://americanradiohistory.com
• Internet Movie Database: The Big Story
http://www.imdb.com/title/tt0041007/fullcredits?ref_=tt_ov_st_sm
• *The Professor and the Coed: Scandal and Murder at the Ohio State University* by Mark Gribben

Paperback Parade #85
Review by Rudolph Schmidt

Since 1986, editor Gary Lovisi has produced *Paperback Parade* through publisher Gryphon Books. It's billed as the world's leading and longest-running magazine on vintage and collectible paperback books, including foreign editions. Each issue of this digest features 100 or more pages of articles on paperback book authors, publishers, series, interviews, a generous helping of cover reproductions, notable facts of interest to collectors, and more.

As a first-time reader of the title, *Paperback Parade* #85 went beyond a pleasant surprise. A single issue was enough to get me hooked. One peek inside the gaudy covers (displayed in full color for the first time in this edition's interior pages), of the dark tales this periodical examines was hardly enough. I subscribed shortly after reading the issue cover-to-cover.

As a relative newcomer to my particular interest, Paperback Original crime fiction, every article in *Paperback Parade* #85 was part discovery, part education. The mix of old and new pulp and paper-

back coverage in Lovisi's introduction, his conversational tone, and the extensive collection of cover artwork—with select iterations—was a thrill ride comparable to some of the best PBOs I've read.

The magazine devotes its pages to a wide range of genre fiction, including crime and mystery, horror, fantasy and science fiction, espionage and sleaze. An overview of the issue's contents follows:

J. Calvitt Clarke III reminisces about his grandfather's novels in the issue's lead and highlight. His inside access and insights into Dr. J. Calvitt Clarke's work provides a compelling profile of the writer's career and how even genre novels are shaped and influenced by an individual's beliefs and the culture of their era. If Clarke III wasn't a direct relation, one might question that the grandfather, writing his later work as Richard Grant, was even the same person, the contrast of styles between his early romance work and his later hardboiled novels is so stark. It's a fascinating article, with a full bibliography.

Jon D. Swartz' tribute piece, dedicated to the memory of Neal Barrett, Jr. provide readers a glimpse into the lifetime of the science fiction and fantasy writer, profusely illustrated with paperback book covers from Lancer, Ace, Daw and others.

A two-page spread, "Cover Swipe," depicts an original 1960's *Jack the Ripper* book cover, painter unknown, and a Spanish-language movie poster with a less-polished "swipe" of the original.

Dale Brumfeld's "Poetic Injustice" profiles the life and work of beat poet Rik Davis. A true outsider, Davis pursued his serious poetry writing under his own name, while often supporting himself writing porn novels (like *Passion's Greatest Trap* shown on the issue's cover) as Jack Vast. His unsolved murder in the bathroom of the B&T Adult Bookstore where he worked in Richmond, Virginia, in 1982,

ended his life tragically at age 43.

Jim Fitzpatrick reports on Guy Endore's *The Werewolf of Paris*, considered to be one of the greatest horror novels ever written, and the basis for the 1961 movie starring Oliver Reed, *The Curse of the Werewolf.*

The list of sources cited for Ed Lynskey's profile of writer Bruno Fischer is nearly half the length of the article itself, so I'll conclude we may never know much about Fischer outside of his over two dozen novels written from 1939 to 1974. Nevertheless, he's considered one of the great crime fiction writers of his era and overdue for a revival of interest in his work.

The issue concludes with fond recollections of fiction favorites in "Hard-Boiled Paradise," by Gary Lovisi. A friendly recount of lesser-known works that deserve a second look. It builds with each successive story highlighted, starting with *One is a Lonely Number* by Bruce Elliott and ending with *Sin Pit* by Paul S. Meskil.

It appears *Paperback Parade* is printed on demand on a nice quality, bright white paper stock. However this edition, weighing in at 104 pages is a bit too much for its saddle-stitch binding, which leaves it bulging, virtually unable to lay flat. It measures 5 1/2" x 8 1/2" and retails for $15. Fortunately, Gryphon switched to perfect binding on the following issue (#86).

Visit Gryphon Books online for *Paperback Parade* subscription information or to order from their selection of back issues (it sells out quickly). And while you're there check out their selection of other books and publications. gryphonbooks.com

Myron Fass: Foto-rama and His Other Digests 1956–1976

Article by Tom Brinkmann

The 1950s

In the 1950s, three decades before the publication of the groundbreaking book *Apocalypse Culture* (editor Adam Parfrey, 1987), Myron Fass started his prolific publishing career, which I would call "Early Apocalypse Culture." Fass edited and published magazines, tabloids, and quite a few digest-sized magazine titles for nearly three decades. And, the digests were some of his earliest publications. Fass acquired the habit of resurrecting titles, published by others, that had gone belly-up and using them on the digests he edited and/or published.

The story starts in New York City's "Printing District," which was at the time, on the lower west-side of Manhattan, or "West-Soho," on Hudson and Varick Streets, which run parallel, north to Houston Street and south to Canal Street, which puts them near the entrance to the Holland Tunnel that takes you to and from New Jersey, into the booming metropolis, that was and is, the City of New York.

The first issue of the digest (approximately 5" x 7") *Foto-rama* was dated January 1953 which pre-dated *Playboy*'s first issue of December 1953. Earlier, there had been an oversized (10 1/4" x 13") mag titled *Foto Parade* which launched their first issue, dated December 1949, with Marilyn Monroe as the covergirl, *Foto-rama*'s title may have been inspired by it. *Foto-rama* was published bi-monthly by Arena Publishing Corporation at 799 Broadway, New York 3, NY. The cover price was twenty-five cents and it was distributed by ACE. *Foto-rama* was one-hundred thirty-two printed pages, sub-titled "The Photo Magazine of Headline Features." Originally, *Foto-rama*'s Editor/Publisher was Michael Estrin with William Harris as the Business Manager.

Wm. Harris was the father of Stanley R. Harris who became Myron Fass' partner in the publishing business a few years later and, remained so until the latter half of 1977 when they had a none too amiable falling out over Fass' underhanded business practices. Stanley Harris went on to form

Foto-rama June 1957.

the successful Harris Publications; while Fass and his brother Irving were brought to court over their four million dollar debt to their printer, Quad Graphics. Irving Fass eventually spilled the beans on his brother's playing games with the distributor's advances, which Myron never forgave him for. Myron started throwing magazines together from previously published magazines (i.e., doing pick-up mags) and moved his business to New Jersey under the SJ Publications name; while his brother Irving started to publish a handful of magazines himself in the late '80s, unsuccessfully. Irving Fass committed suicide in Florida in 1991.

The early *Foto-rama* did indeed have some interesting articles and features, which of course, were always packed with photos. The cover blurbs on the first issue held promise, "The Rawest Night Club in the U.S.," "Meet Rocky Marciano," and "Zsa Zsa Gabor UNDRESSES!" The second issue (March 1953)

offered up: "I Am A B-Girl," and inside had articles and photos on "Collecting Book Matches" by Leon Thiels; an extensive article on "Disc Jockeys Moguls of Music" by David Taylor Marke; "Spiritualism America's Biggest Fake Business Exposed!"; "Hellfire" on the historic Hellfire Club in England, and so on.

Foto-rama's sixth issue (November 1953) had a gem of an article: "Occult Artist Draws Visions from A Mystic World" which was about the obscure, New Zealand-born, Australian artist Rosaleen Norton who made a slight splash in the early fifties with the publication of her unique book *The Art of Rosaleen Norton* (1952). In fact, later on, none other than Forrest J. Ackerman himself wrote the article "Burn, Witch, Burn!" in the second issue of the magazine *Sex and Censorship* (1958) about Ms. Norton and her book, which I wrote about in the second volume of my book *Bad Mags*.

Eventually, *Foto-rama* was published with its editorial offices at 225 Varick Street. And, by 1956, the editor was listed as Abner J. Sundell, which sounds like a pseudonym to me but, I just can't say for sure. Neither Irving Fass nor Mel Lenowitz were listed in the masthead yet. Many of the issues from the fifties had well-known femmes on the covers, such as: Betty Page (4/55), Eve Meyer (6/57), Tina Louise (7/58, 12/59), and Candy Barr (1/59), which were just a few of the early covergirls, who also had photo layouts inside.

Myron Fass was first listed as *Foto-rama*'s Editor starting sometime in late 1956, by that time he had edited and/or published a handful of magazines such as *Lunatickle*,

True Problems, and *Ogle*. *Foto-rama* was Fass's first and longest running digest magazine which he kept going for two decades. By the time Myron Fass started editing *Foto-rama* its distributor had changed from ACE to Publishers Distribution Company (PDC). In my humble opinion, the best issues of *Foto-rama* were from the fifties. And, a great example was the March 1957 issue, which had the blurb, "Ghouls Exploit James Dean," across the bottom of the cover. Of course, Myron was doing that very thing by using that cover blurb and story but, not in quite the same way that the article accused "ghouls" in Los Angeles and New York of profiting from Dean's demise by bilking teenagers of "hundreds of thousands of dollars." The piece lists some of the items offered for sale to beware of: "1) Dean's unpublished poems, written in his own hand; 2) pieces of the car he died in; 3) Dean's death mask; 4) furniture from Dean's Hollywood apartment, or any possessions reputedly belonging to the dead actor." Besides the four-page Dean article, the issue contained other amazing features such as, "Fool's Paradise" three pages of Fass cartoons; a five-page Lili St. Cyr feature; an eight-page Diane Webber layout; photos of Anita Eckberg and, to top it all off "Why Betty Loves It!" that was six pages of Betty Page posing and quoted as saying, "There's not too much I'd rather do than pose for pic-

tures."; the feature "Does Chita Ever Cheat?" was "your favorite editor" Myron Fass with Chita Rivera that was put together with photos culled from *Ogle*'s first issue, March 1956, and in an ad for *Ogle*, the copy read "*Ogle* magazine—sex with a giggle—at your favorite newstand [sic]."

The Eve Meyer cover on the June 1957 issue was one of, if not the, best cover to grace *Foto-rama*, her facial expression, not to mention her amazing bosom, were priceless! And, Ms. Meyer had a six-page photo layout inside as well, with the photos taken by her husband Russ, of course. Then, there was the inexplicable juxtaposition of the two cover blurbs, "Why Girls Get Raped!" which was next to Ms. Meyer and "Presley Gets De-sexed" which was underneath her bosom. The issue also carried a two-page "Fool's Paradise" feature which had a cartoon of a pot-bellied policeman, who looked suspiciously like Fass, listening to a woman, clothed only in bra and gloves, tell him "I dreamed I was pinched in my Maidenform bra!"

The November 1958 issue of *Foto-rama* had the blond-bombshell covergirl, Shirley Houser, wrapped up in what looked like a shiny red satin show-girl thingy and fishnet stockings. Ms. Houser also appeared on another *Foto-rama* cover (12/60) and in "The Case of the Purple Woman" episode of *Perry Mason* as a waitress that year, and

> "Ms. Houser also appeared . . . in 'The Case of the Purple Woman' episode of *Perry Mason* as a waitress that year, and was also in a show in Las Vegas."

Foto-rama Nov. 1958.

was also in a show in Las Vegas. On this particular cover there was a one-and-three-quarter-inch banner across most of her legs that read "Monsters-Vampires Horror Contest" with the words "Big Money Prizes" on either side. Proof positive that editor Myron loved his monsters. The "big money" first prize was $250—remember this was 1958. The actual contest consisted of eight photos of monsters from films which the contestant had to name, and then identify the actor that portrayed the monster, and name the film it came from. The second part was writing, "In 50 words or less, tell us why you like monster movies." The issue also had a color fold-out of Claire Fitzpatrick, backed with a black-and-white photo of covergirl Shirley Houser.

Photo Life's first issue was dated October 1958 and was published bi-monthly by Lux Publications, Inc. from 225 Varick Street, New York 14, NY. The cover price was thirty-five cents and it was a digest with one-hundred thirty-six printed pages. The Editor was listed as "Norym Shaf" which was an early Fass pseudonym—read the two names backwards. One of the other credits given was a name that would show up in Myron's magazines again and again was Mel Lenowitz, Research Editor; not only would Lenowitz show up again (sometimes as Mel Lenny) but, he was a constant, who stayed with Fass, fulfilling various jobs, until the early 1980s. In the premiere issue was a color fold-out of Jayne Mansfield and, subsequent issues also contained color fold-outs. *Photo Life* lasted into the early sixties but I haven't been able to pin it down to a specific year. Although, you could find an ad which offered four back issues of *Foto-rama* and *Photo Life* for one dollar in other Fass digests up to and including the year 1967.

A year later, the *Photo Life* of October 1959 had an amazing photo-filled five-page feature on TV horror hostess Vampira titled "Does She Suck Blood?" And, I guess in honor of it being the Halloween month issue, another feature called, "Why

Photo Life Oct. 1959.

You Enjoy Having the Hell Scared Out of You," about the popularity of horror movies, which included a photo of Zacherly, another TV horror host. *Photo Life* asked the question to horror movie fans and a New York psychiatrist, James E. Vance, who clued everybody in as to why we enjoy horror, with his answer, "It's sort of a sex substitute and an entirely innocuous one." Vance continued on saying, "It is curious that women see personified in the 'beast' unbridled sex which they secretly covet yet are frightened of." Which was countered by Bill Johnson, a movie fan saying, "I dig horror movies and I'm no girl. They are entertaining, what else can I say?" The issue's color fold-out was Jayne Mansfield, who also had a photo feature titled "Jayne's Nude In Vegas."

The 1960s

In some issues of *Foto-rama* from the early 1960s, the Editor was listed as "Ron Mass" another

Ladies Home Companion July 1965.

early Fass pseudonym, while his brother Irving Fass was listed as Art Director. In another issue from 1963 the Editor was listed as R. Simms Madison who was, in 1961, in the masthead in charge of "Production."

Foto-rama's March 1961 cover informed people that Jayne Mansfield was really a brunette with a cover photo to prove it, and the blurb, "Proof: Jayne Mansfield Is Really A Brunette!" With the cover spoiler out of the way, the feature inside was titled, "Is Mansfield Brunet [sic]?" The opening blurb stated, "You've seen the screen's sex bombshell as a blonde and a brunette both . . . . what's her real shade? Don't ask how we know . . . . but jolting Jayne is really a jet tresser!"

The same issue from 1961 had one of the most factual and succinct articles I have ever read on LSD, titled, "The Drug That Drives Girls Wild!" The intro blurb said it all, "They call it everything from 'Hot Juice' to 'Wild,' but the real name of the new sex drug being smuggled

into this country from Communist China is LSD." There was some priceless dialogue in the short article, forgive me for indulging in it. After a woman had been given some LSD in a drink, I quote her, "'I'm hot!' she yelled suddenly—'hot all over—hot—hot—and I want to get hotter!'" And then, "'Push my panic button again,' she laughed, 'push it, play with it and use it, and make me flip! I'm flying to mattressville!'"

Foto-rama's November 1963 issue had another interesting Mansfield cover blurb and inside article on the "Untold Story Behind Sabrina-Mansfield Feud," or "Busts A-Poppin' . . . The Sabrina-Mansfield Feud," the title of the piece inside. Sabrina (Norma Ann Sykes) was the British version of a Mansfield-type, blonde bombshell, glamour girl. The readers were given Sabrina's and Jayne's measurements. Sabrina's: height, 5 feet 6 1/2 inches; chest, 42; waist, 23; hips, 38; weight, 127 pounds. Jayne's: height, 5 feet 5 3/4 inches; chest, 41; waist, 20; hips, 35 1/2; weight, 118 pounds. Sabrina must have trained her waist with a corset, as I have read elsewhere that it was a wasp-like 19 inches, and it looks it in the photos. Sabrina worked a crowd "on all her sex cylinders" the readers were told, while Jayne used her cleavage at its best when bending over, towards the camera. The question was posed, "Who can out-cleavage who?" Sabrina seems to have been the challenger, claiming she would meet Jayne anywhere, any time and give her the "choice of weapons: bikini, evening dress, sweater or you name it." Jayne ignored it all, and kept silent.

In the same issue, you would also find a great full-page ad offering all three issues of Fass's 1962 *Thriller* horror mags for one dollar! A well advised investment in hindsight, as they all fetch high prices today on the collector's market. The ad was complete with a paragraph-length come-on replete with the word "weird" misspelled that read: "A wierd [sic] and wild collection of gals and ghouls guaranteed to send shivers down your spine and scare the yell out of you. Find out how it feels to make love to a vampire, date a she-devil, learn about the strange love practices of the occult, the wicked and wanton ways of a fetching witch, meet the gal who'd like somebody to lay her in her grave! It's horriffic! These are giant 8 1/2 x 11 inch books!"

PIC Dec. 1963.

The original *Ladies Home Companion* was a magazine title from the turn-of-the-century, until Myron Fass decided to do a digest for the ladies. You might be saying, "Myron Fass did a magazine for women?" Well, Myron Fass did multitudes of titles you might not expect, they weren't all sleazy, sordid stuff. He also published magazine titles such as: *American Horseman, Today's Jogger, Dogs, Countrywide Sports, Popular Guns, Outdoor Sports Life, Air Aces, Vette Power, High Performance Rods*, and so on, and on, and on.

Ladies Home Companion was resurrected by Fass in 1962, as the earliest issue I've seen is March 1963 (v1 #5) which would indicate that. In that same issue, was a fourteen-page feature titled "Silence Please!" which was "a special plea to every decent American woman regarding the new unfounded Kennedy family rumors . . ." It was fortuitous timing on Myron Fass' part, to cash in on the Kennedy's Camelot White House

and, a year later, after JFK's assassination. Myron was on it—*LHC's* February 1964 issue had Sophia Loren and her husband Carlo Ponti as the cover couple but, it also had a silver inset with black type on it, made to look like a sticker but, which had been printed as part of the cover, that read: "President Kennedy's Last Day In the White House EXCLUSIVE PHOTOS." The May 1964 issue was the "Special Kennedy Issue," and the cover showed the first couple together in what looked to be the White House, the blurbs read: "Johnson and Jackie in '64: Her Plan To Run For Vice President"—"JFK's Last Message To Children"—"When They Were Newly Weds: Exclusive: Their First Year Together." The July 1965 issue had Jackie on the cover once again, next to the top blurb, "Jackie and the Man From Mexico."

The title *"Pic"* had been around since the 1930s, originally with quotation marks around it, later

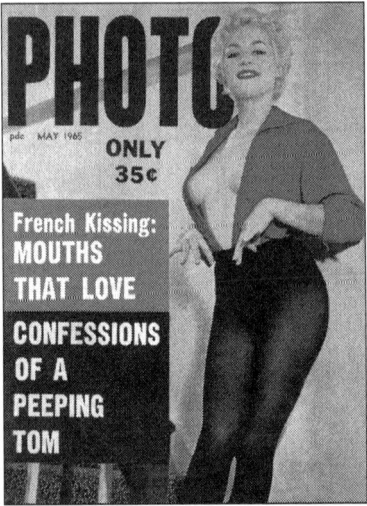

Photo May 1965.   Companion April 1966.

without them, but had gone through at least a couple of publishers, including Street & Smith, before Fass decided to use it. *Pic* was a digest Fass first published in December of 1963, the first issue was a gem, with a classic note from the Editor ("Rochelle Davis") opening up the mag, printed on top of a classic photo which showed Sammy Davis, Jr. sitting with a bunch of white guys watching a stripper on stage shaking her hootchie-koo. The photo was in connection to a cover blurb and article titled, "Sammy Davis, Jr. and the French Nude." The editorial note read:

"*PIC* brings you a brand new look at life on the seamless side—we cover and uncover all the action, wherever the action is: in Paris with Sammy (mostly rearguard there), in London with Chris (front and side views, up and down action), all over the world, where the girls are. That's the ticket, now let's enjoy the ride! The Editor"

The "Chris" referred to in the

above quote was the covergirl, Christine Keeler, a British call girl whose clientele were members of Parliament, and featured in the article "Christine Wants More Men." The female editor, "Rochelle Davis," was a gimmick that did not last long. In the October 1965 issue the editor was listed as Charles Hayden, and eventually it was Frank Uberti, *Foto-rama*'s editor.

The first digest titled *Photo* had been around since 1952 and was published monthly by Official Magazine Corporation located at 270 Park Avenue in New York, not far from where Myron Fass would end up in the 1970s. Fass' *Photo* was launched in 1964, the editor listed in the May 1965 issue was Leonard Miller. *Photo* was published monthly by Tempest Publications, another of Fass' many imprints.

Companion, formerly *Ladies Home Companion*, had its title shortened sometime from late 1965 to early 1966, as the first issue I've seen as *Companion* is February

1966. It was not a change in name only but, also content. The concern with celebrities and the Kennedys were gone and *Companion* began to take a more serious look at the problems of sex and relationships, many of its articles written by doctors. For example let's take a look at the cover blurbs from the April 1966 issue of *Companion*, "Should A Wife Close Her Eyes to Adultery," "Children Who Hate Their Parents," "A High School Teacher Talks About Teen-age Homosexuality," and "Why Single Girls Prefer Married Men." You could say it was sort of a poor man's *Sexology*. In 1967 celebrity crept back in slightly, as the October '67 issue had an article titled, "Sharon Tate—Ready Made Star" by Roy Mosny, who was a writer that wrote for Fass for a few decades and eventually edited Fass' digest *People Today* a couple of years later. The article related the story of how Tate's beauty embarrassed her but, ultimately opened doors for her until she was "discovered" by Martin Ransohoff, a "star-maker" who had launched the careers of Ann Margaret and Tuesday Weld. Mosny also wrote of Tate's first encounters with her future husband, filmster Roman Polanski, and his bizarre courtship of her in London while hiring her to be in his film *The Fearless Vampire Killers*. In the back of the same issue was the article "Private Life of America's Hippies—An inside look at our new American sub-culture," by Joel Metz, an interesting unintended companion piece to the Sharon Tate article, I would say.

In the April 1969 issue the main cover blurb/article was "SEX and the Supernatural: The Erotic Side of the Occult," by Elijah Hadynn, which

Companion April 1969.

kicked off by saying in the opening blurb, "Sex is an act in which man transcends himself and reality. Why then does he refuse to admit the supernatural aspects of sexuality?" The article was a argument for the belief that two people separated physically by thousands of miles could experience intimate sexual relations simultaneously, and have the ecstatic gyrations of one of the lovers observed by a third party as proof. An example was related of that very phenomena between a soldier fighting in the Pacific in WWII and his girlfriend who was living in San Francisco. Another interesting thing about the issue was the article "Hearse Chasers," by I. Stuart Rosengard, which was also used in the August 1969 issue of *Foto-rama*, with the same photo and layout [described on page 79]. The last date I have seen on an issue of *Companion* is February 1972. I don't know when it went belly up but, my guess would be not long after '72.

By 1966 the editor of *Foto-rama*

Bold Feb. 1968.

was listed as Frank Uberti and Irving Fass was gone from the masthead; the cover did carry Fass' yellow, black, and white Country Wide Publications logo but, Arena Publishing was still listed in the indicia as the publisher, located at 250 Hudson Street. Uberti would continue on as *Foto-rama*'s editor until its demise in 1976. Whether "Frank Uberti" was another Fass pseudonym or not, I do not know but, my guess would be that it was. Fass did have long running pseudonyms such as "Bryant Hall," and for writing "Jack Crandall" which, ex-Fass editor Jeff Goodman tells me, Myron would even use to sign some of his printing contracts!

All the Fass published digests had their titles in bold, sans serif letters, with the exception of *Bold*'s title type which had serifs, and later, *People Today* which was all in lower case letters with serifs. And, in 1966 all the sex digest titles had covers which started to use bright colors for the backgrounds and/or inset boxes. You could say, they were almost psychedelic!

Foto-rama's August 1966 issue had a cover blurb "Grotto of Horror" referring to a feature inside titled "Hollywood's Grotto of Horror" about the new "nightclub sensation" on the corner of Hollywood and Vine called The Haunted House! The "Mad Doctor" that welcomed you into the cavernous club was actually Al Ward, the greeter, wearing a rubber mask. You were well advised not to let the abundance of bats, skulls, shrunken heads, and skeletons hanging around the place rattle you to the point of having to visit a head shrinker! The high point was the monstrous band shell designed into a demonic head with its mouth wide open, pointed teeth gleaming, and nostrils smoking. The monstrous stage prop could be found in certain porn shoots in adult slicks in years to come. Fass was would also occasionally use stills from sixties skin flicks in his magazines later on.

As an example of where *Foto-rama* was at by the end of the sixties let's take a look at an issue from 1969 and, the most infamous month of that year, August. Two cover blurbs screamed in black and red type from the bright yellow background, "The SUCKER Game—Girls Who Play It," "Sweden's Stripping CALL GIRLS—They Show It Before They Sell It," while the third blurb was in white type in a green rectangle at the bottom that read, "Britain's Bang-Bang Clubs." The covergirl was generic and wearing a black lace top, open down the front, with her head tilted sideways and a knowing smirk on her face. I would have to say that the most notable thing about *Foto-rama* at this point was the amount of sleazy sex ads. The one ad that is of primary interest, because it replaced the ad mentioned earlier with back issues of *Foto-rama* and *Photo Life*, was a full-page ad for back issues of all four Fass sex digest titles, saying: "Most Sensational Offer Ever Made—4 of the Most Daring Issues of *Foto-rama*, *Pic*, *Photo* & *Bold* ever printed only $1.00—All Collector's Items—Rare editions—Special offer to Our readers only."

And, in a circular blurb under the above text it added: "Also the first 100 who order will receive 10 exciting nude girlie photos!"

All from, Portrait Enterprises, 150 Fifth Avenue, New York 11, NY.

The other ads in the mag were funnier and sleazier but of less interest, advertising essentials such as the "Big Brown Baby Doll," "Exciting Blonde Negress," "Uncommon Photos," "Jayne Mansfield Filmed Nude," "Offbeat Films," "Lonesome Negro Girl," "Nude Acrobatics," "Privately Printed Mags," "Raised Skirts," "Fabulous Fannies," and so on. There were the articles that made the whole thing "socially redeemable" though. A few of the choice ones, in between the girlie features in the issue were: "Puck Luck" that which keeps a hockey goalies face from looking like a "detailed map"; "Hearse Chasers—The Lowest Racket of Them All" about people being swindled by others scouring the obituaries for victims that included widows and Vietnam Vets' families; "Riots! Riots! Riots!" about student riots taking place all over the globe at the time; and "Bobsled Champs" about the World Bobsled Championship Races being held in Lake Placid, New York.

The original magazine titled *Eye* had the sub-title "People and Pictures" and started out as an oversized (10" x 13") mag and later downsized to a digest, published throughout the fifties by Mutual Magazine Corporation in New York. The Fass digest with the same title, *Eye*, seems to have been launched at the end of 1966, and had no sub-title. The Fass *Eye* didn't seem to have lasted very long. The reason I keep using the word "seem" is that I only have one issue of it to go on, the July 1967 issue (volume 1, #6) and it wasn't one of the digests Fass was still publishing in the 1970s. It was published bi-monthly, cost thirty-five cents and, was one-hundred printed pages. The Editor was listed as Paul Kenilworth, with the Associate Editor as Maury Swift—the same exact staff as *Bold*. The publisher was listed as Stories, Layouts & Press, Inc., a known Fass imprint. There were two addresses given that were both associated with Fass, 150 Fifth Avenue in New York, and 191 Middlesex Avenue, Englewood Cliffs in New Jersey. The contents were the same type of features found in *Pic*, *Photo*, and *Foto-rama*.

The first use of the title *Bold* was on a "pocket magazine" (approx. 4" x 6") published monthly by Enterprise Magazine Management Inc., from 381 Fourth Avenue, New York 16, NY, since the early 1950s. The Fass *Bold* was sleazy sex from its start in 1967 and, as mentioned above, listed the same staff in the masthead as *Eye*. *Bold* was published by Fass' Stories, Layouts & Press, Inc., imprint and completed the four sex digest titles (along with *Foto-rama*, *Pic*, and *Photo*) of Country Wide Publications that would last until 1976. *Eye* and *Companion* didn't seem to

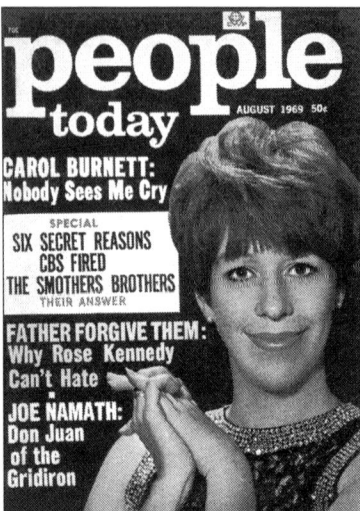

People Today Aug. 1969.

last that long into the seventies.

The title *People Today* "A Magazine About Headline People" was originally used on the long running "pocket magazine," (4.25" x 6") which was published bi-weekly by Hillman Periodicals, Inc., from 535 Fifth Avenue, New York 17, NY. The first issue was dated June 20, 1950 and it continued throughout the 1950s, and into the early '60s. *People Today* was also the last digest title (5.25" x 7") that Fass resurrected, and was launched with the August 1969 issue that had Carol Burnett on the cover. This first resurrection of Fass' *People Today* was published by his imprint, Ladies Coronet, Inc., 222 Park Avenue South, New York. The masthead included—Myron Fass as Publisher; Roy Mosny, Editor; Irving Fass, Executive Art Director; Stanley Harris, Business Manager; Mel Lenny, Advertising Representative. The curious thing about Mel Lenny's listed job in the first issue, is that there was not a single ad in the book! There were

articles on "Carol Burnett—Nobody Sees Me Cry," "The Dating Rules Tricia Nixon Follows," "Peggy Fleming—The Girl With The Silver Skates," "Rona Barrett: The Secret Code of A Hollywood Snoop," and more. The fifth issue (June 1970) had Goldie Hawn as the covergirl/main feature with "The Glitter of Goldie Hawn—She's A Lovable Kook—With A Golden Touch." And another article titled, "Charles Manson: The Alleged Murderer Who Thought He Was the Angel of Death" which was fairly empathetic towards Manson's childhood circumstances. But, the anonymous writer then came up with creative phrases for Manson such as: "a cardboard John the Baptist disguised as a hippie," "a demon lover," and "a Pied Piper of sorts, leading lost children so far away they [would] never be able to come back again." Because of the timing of Fass' launch of this title, August 1969, the very month the Tate/LaBianca murders occurred, I can only assume that issues two, three, and four might have had articles on them before this Manson article. But, unfortunately, I have never seen those issues. Other features in the issue were: "Jane Fonda: An Outsider To Her Own Country," "Tricia Nixon: The Mystery Girl In The White House," "The Many Worlds of Leonard Nimoy," and "Liza Minnelli: 'When Can I Be Me?'" I have no clue what happened to *People Today* beyond the fifth issue, as it is hard to find any issues of this Fass title.

People Today was resurrected a second time by Fass when he was in Florida in 1994–95, publishing as Scope Publications, Inc., from Ft. Lauderdale. But, it was titled *People Today Secrets* and, was an all-glossy, 8.5" x 11" mag, in emulation of *People Weekly*. This last reincarnation had such notables as Sharon Stone, The Rolling Stones, and Pam Anderson on the covers. It was one of the last magazines published by Myron Fass.

The 1970s

I won't get into detailed descriptions of the digests from the 1970s but, some of the cover blurbs are an indication: "Chicks Who Dig Big Tools," "Doing What Comes Unnaturally," "Banging Bondage Babes," "Broads Who Come With A Whipping," "Bicentennial Babes Who Can Blow Your Horn," "The Whack and Crack Parlors of the S&M Freaks," "Hot Flesh Games For Lesbians Only," and so on. In 1975–76 the ban on showing nipples on the covers of magazines was lifted, for a short time, therefore, the last Fass digests published had bare breasted women on their covers. It seems that the four mainstay Fass sex digests pulled through until 1976 by all indications. I know that *Foto-rama*, *Pic*, and *Photo* did for sure, *Bold* is the only question mark. The last date I can confirm for *Bold* is 1974, but, I would be willing to bet it made it until 1976 also.

By 1977 the Fass published digest titles were all history. In fact, that form of digest, the 5" x 7", magazine had all but disappeared. The publishers of *Penthouse*, *Club*, *Velvet*, *Swank*, *Oui*, *Chic*, and various other glossy girlie mags started their own 5.5" x 8.5" digest titles that Fass never tried to compete with; titles like *Penthouse Forum*, *Penthouse Variations*, *Penthouse Hot Talk*, *Swank's Erotic Letters*, *Club Quest*, *Human Digest*, *Velvet Touch*, *Velvet's*

Eye July 1967.

Vibrations, and so on, which were printed on glossy paper in color; the later two titles, Jeff Goodman eventually would edit after he left his job editing for Fass early in 1979. In the 1980s, sex digest titles multiplied like mushrooms and got kinkier and sleazier, and most had their insides printed on newsprint; titles such as *Pocketfox*, *Original Letters*, *Forbidden Letters*, *Hot & Sexy*, *Uncensored Letters*, *X Letters*, ad infinitum.

Myron Fass was a unique individual and prolific publisher. And, he was one of the last old-time pulp publishers from that era. He published hundreds of titles over the span of almost four decades, from 1956–1995. He died September 14, 2006 in Ft. Lauderdale, Florida.

Tom Brinkmann writes about unusual periodicals at: www.badmags.com His books *Bad Mags* vol. 1 and 2 are available on Amazon. He writes for *Headpress Journal* (UK) and publishes the *On the Rack* zine. For details contact him at: tom@badmags.com

A Foul Breath of Fresh Air

Crime fiction by Richard Krauss
Illustrated by Michael Neno

"There are seven different kinds of murder. Which kind all comes down to intent. The intent you can sell." Eddie peered down from the top bunk, legs dangling over the edge.

My last night in lockup. One more sweaty night in the bowels of hell. I'd heard it before, but anything to bust up the endless boredom inside was okay by me.

"You're screwed if the charge is first degree. That means you planned it, like a hit. Automatic life—or

death, depending on the state. Second degree is more spontaneous. It wasn't part of the plan, but you had to make adjustments along the way."

Eddie was hanging onto middle age with two down on a seven-year jolt. He'd learned how to chit-chat

the dickwads on both sides of the iron. If he kept his cool he'd be out in a year or two. Meantime, he had a job he was pushing me to take.

"If you kill somebody during a felony crime—like dealing or armed robbery, it's felony murder."

Eddie was the best frenemy I'd made inside. When the wolves spot a twenty-something greener like me, they get juiced. Putting up with Eddie's bullshit was worth it, to draft off his rep. When I got out, he wanted me to snuff some dude. Had everything laid out.

"Third degree, or manslaughter, splits in two directions. Voluntary is the heat of the moment. Like the poor fool who walks in on his girlfriend banging his best friend. Involuntary is by accident, 'cept they put on it you, like a DUI that ends up in a sidewalk shrine."

I'd say Eddie's still pretty sharp for late-stage boomer. But he screwed up on his second bank job. Tried to pull it off too close to a unmarked Crown Vic. Never even showed the passaround he had on him. Didn't matter. Holding made it armed robbery, worth seven long. But murder.

Fuck me, that's a whole 'nother thing. No way I'm going there.

"You can even get away with it. War is the best example. But self-defense can work. Or mercy killing, where you put some schmuck out of his misery. Perfectly legal in places like Oregon."

As he spewed his lesson, I paced all ten feet of our cell, from stainless steel crapper to iron bars. "I got only one intention," I said. "Get out and never come back."

"Yup, you had a tough eighteen months all right, pulled over on a shoplift and nailed for possession, and transporting a piece. Shit. Be nice and quiet around here without your bellyaching."

"Fuck you. By tomorrow, I'll forget about your sorry ass every day, between shots of Cuervo and getting laid."

Eddie's face went sour. He was more fat than muscle, but still, he was way bigger than me. I felt my shoulders cinch up as he slid himself down to the floor. I backed off a step, but where you gonna go in a prison cell? He caught hold of my arm, twisted it behind me and shoved my face into the side of the upper bunk. Then he leaned in close. I felt his foul breath on my ear, a whaft of chicken and stale coffee from the evening's mess. "Tonight's our last night together, Jackie. Maybe I should make you beg me for it."

I tried to break his grip, but he jerked my arm up, shooting a jolt of pure agony across my shoulder. He licked the tip of my ear and smacked his lips. Then, as suddenly as he'd grabbed me, he let go, shoving me into the lower bunk with his foot. When I turned over, he was grinning. "Puss, puss, puss," he whispered through puckered lips.

I rubbed my shoulder and glared up at him as he loomed over me.

"Eighteen months in the can and you still ain't learned a damn thing. See, you don't earn respect in here, puss, you take it. Next time you're inside," he leaned forward to dig his knuckle into my chest, "no more coddling. It's all gonna be on you."

Then he went back into his pitch. "You wanna be a bad ass, take out that guy Hutchison, like I told you. Guy like that will never be missed. Take his stash, then burn him out to cover your tracks."

He really wanted me to snuff this guy.

"As much as I'm gonna miss our little chats," I said, "I haven't decided what I'll do. Maybe get a gig at the lumber yard or the truck plant in Portland." I thought maybe that would tweak him a little, but he just shook his head and climbed back up to his pulpit.

"Yeah, you do that. Once they catch wind you did time for holding crank and an unregistered semi, the only job you'll ever get is one they can't give away." He bent forward, smirking at me. "You're a lifer, Jack. A tool. You just don't know it yet."

When he got pissed, Eddie sounded just like my old man, Cy. Same bullshit, different asshole.

I angled out of my bunk to get a clear view of him. "Look, I'm gonna need some wheels, dude. Can you hook me up or what?"

Eddie fixed his gaze on me, his lips pulled back as if trying to cover a grin. "Sure thing. Get yourself in touch with my man Marco, Marco Juvera. Owns a joint called Rapid Pawn in north Portland, St. Johns area. He'll get you going."

"Thanks for setting me up. I owe you one."

In the morning, Eddie and I traded no goodbyes. I left him my iPod, shampoo, toothpaste and some other crap, anyway. It was as good as cash, inside.

Then I was gone. They shuffled me around to rooms I'd never seen before. Had me sign papers. It really started to take hold when I slipped into the street clothes they gave me. Then they led me through three sets of barred doors. Each one opening wide.

There's really no way to describe the feeling of getting out. The whole fucking world is waiting for you.

Ma was there for me just like she promised. Always had my back. If you'da seen us, you woulda seen nothing but ivory. She wrapped her arms around me and started bawlin'; happy as hell. Almost got me going too.

We headed for the car. She couldn't keep her hands off me, rubbing my back, tilting her head onto my shoulder. "I'm so happy you're finally coming home, Jack."

"Feels like I could do anything," I said.

We were both lit up pretty damn good, just on the fucking moment. Ridiculous.

She still had the white Maxima. Looked exactly the same as the last time I saw it almost two years ago. Like the world froze, waiting for me to return. "You take the day off for this?" I asked her.

"Just the morning," she said as she unlocked the car. "I wish we had time to stop and eat, but I have to be back by one o'clock and it's over an hour's drive from here."

As we pulled out onto the road, I spun my head around so I could watch the Pen shrink behind us.

"The free ride is over."

"You still working for Devlin?"

"Yes, thank goodness. It's been a tough year. Construction is really slow right now. Thank the Lord they still need a bookkeeper."

"They're lucky to have you."

"It's tough out there. The economy still hasn't recovered. Not many companies are hiring. You're going to have to work to find something."

"I get what you're saying, but just being out in the world, just being free, I've got no worries today." We hit the on-ramp to the Five, going north. It felt amazing to see the world flying past all around.

"Jack, you know I'm happy for you," she said, her voice all business now. "But you can't go on like before. You've got to turn your life around. Go ahead and take a few days to unwind. But then you need to get serious about your future. Straighten yourself out and find a legitimate job. I'm giving you thirty days. Then you'll need to find someplace else to stay."

"What? I just got sprung. Like, ten minutes ago."

"Look, this hasn't been easy for either one of us. I'm just doing what I should've done two years ago. Then maybe none of this would've ever happened."

"Is that what this is about— my arrest? I did my time on that, remember? Why are you busting my chops already?"

"Jack, you're almost 23 years old. It's time you straightened yourself out. The free ride is over. You can't let your past mistakes ruin your future. Everyone agrees on it."

"Jesus, listen to you. Who you been talking to?"

"No! This is about you. Not me, not anyone else."

"I just want to know where this is coming from."

"Oh, for God's sake. It's coming from you! What you've done with your life the last six, seven years. It has to stop. Can't you see that?"

"Whatever." I folded my arms across my chest and turned toward the window. I'd never seen her like this before. What timing.

We drove the rest of the way pretty much in silence. Her, glaring at the road ahead. Me, looking out the window, trying to take what I could from the view.

I admit I've had some trouble, but it's mostly been bad luck; like the first time at MacClaren. Broke some punk's face for hitting on my girlfriend. If the little prick's parents hadn't insisted on pressing charges . . . Chick ended up dumping me anyway. Said she couldn't handle a boyfriend in juvie hall.

Did my second bit at MacClaren for cleaning out the till at the Rose Valley Market. Chump change, barely a hundred bucks. Anybody else would've got a warning, but the cops had it in for me 'cause of my old man, who had a long run of near misses. They were happy to nail anybody with a last name of Langer.

But the Pen was different. The worst. I'll never go back there again. Everybody inside is just trying to find a way to get through. Some are pissed off 24/7, so nobody gets in their business. Some work on their bods all day long. Some get religion. I had Eddie. Eddie wasn't really all that bad ass, but he was smart. He knew how to come off hard case. I was lucky we hooked up.

After a few miles, I looked over at Ma. She took it bad when I got sent to MacClaren the second time. I knew that, but I never thought about what my time in a real prison would do to her. She was harder now. Wrung out and angry. Like when Dad burned her. Guess my last "one more chance" had finally arrived.

As we neared St. Helens, I tried a new angle. "Are you seeing anybody these days?"

She shot me one of her looks. "Don't you remember I wrote you about Bob, Steve Temkin's brother?"

The Temkins had always been good neighbors to us, in spite of my old man. "Yeah right, Bob Temkin. You said he works at the Armstrong plant, right? So how serious is this?"

"Yes, he's the foreman there. We're both just taking things slow, for now. Getting to know one another."

"Good for you. You guys ever talk about me?"

"I don't hide your record from people. It's better to talk things out. I keep trying to figure out how to help you get back on the straight and narrow."

"No worries there. I'm never doing time again."

As we pulled into the lot at Devlin's, I said, "Let me have the keys while you're at work." I needed to hook up with Marco to get myself back in the groove.

Ma killed the engine and handed me the keys. "I'm off at five o'clock. Stay out of trouble."

"No worries, I'm just gonna hang out for awhile. Can you spot me a twenty?"

It felt great to get behind the wheel again. I headed south to Scappoose for a pit stop at Carson's on my way to Portland. Got me the classic with o-rings and fries and a big 'ol strawberry shake. Best meal I'd had in years. Old lady Carson herself brought it over. Never much to look at, she was seriously raisined up now. Gave me the full ex-con treatment. Sugar-coated smiley, with a side of dagger eye.

The gas gauge in the Maxima told me I could hang onto my last five bucks, so I headed down to the St. Johns hood in north Portland and cruised for street life. A dude at a camera shop put me onto Trumbull St. Once I had that, Marco Juvera's place was easy.

The name RAPID PAWN was lit up in red neon inside the front window of a two-story building that had once been painted white. Its windows imprisoned by tightly-spaced, dirty white bars.

There was a loud buzz when I threw the door open, and it kept buzzing till the door swung shut behind me. A long display case, directly across from the entry, was packed with jewelry, cameras, coins and other shiny objects.

"How may I help you?" asked the old guy behind the counter. He was doing about sixty, and it didn't look easy. Face was dark and chewed-up from something in his past. Hair was long and gray, and mostly behind him. He stared at me through two dark slits.

"I'm looking for Marco," I said.

"Regrettably, he's not currently available. Perhaps I can assist you. Do you have something to pawn or are you here for redemption?" The left side of his face cracked a smile as he settled his forearms onto the counter.

"I need to talk to Marco," I said. "Guy named Eddie Walker told me Marco would set me up."

Leatherface straightened up and seemed lost for a minute, fondling his beard. I guess the dots finally connected. "Please excuse me for a moment. I think I may have heard him return by means of the back entry."

He disappeared through a curtain behind the counter, so I took a sec to look around. The walls were packed with TVs, guitars, electronics, trophies, and a ton of other crap. To the right was a gun safe. Open, with some nice whammies inside. Just looking, thanks. I knew I couldn't go there again. Besides, if I needed a weapon, I should still have a six-inch hunting blade back at Ma's place.

Leatherface reappeared and gestured toward the curtain, "Marco has indeed returned to his office now. You may proceed."

Marco Juvera was seated behind a computer in a small office crammed full of stuff that looked like it ought to be out in the shop. A stocky chicano with buzz-cut black hair, matching goatee and a baby Jesus tattoo on his right forearm. Looked maybe 50.

When he heard me come in, he got up to greet me, "Buenos! Jack Langer, right? Eddie told me you was coming." He held out his fist for a bump like we were already old buds. "How's he holding up?"

"You know Eddie," I said. "Tighter than a shit-faced wino. He told me to come see you about a loan. You cool with that?"

He smiled. "All business, eh, Jack Langer? No hay pedo. How much are you looking for?"

"I need a half-way decent car, so I was thinking like five large."

Marco cocked his head, then smiled. "Five grand is a little too grand, amigo. But I'll take a chance on you for one."

"Looks like Eddie sent me to the wrong man. I need at least four."

We stared at each other in silence for a tick. Marco smacked his lips. "I see you're a man who knows what he wants. I'll tell you what, since Eddie spoke for you, I'll make it two. Money's tight, so that's my best deal."

"If you can do two, you can do three."

"Take two or we're done here."

I took it.

Marco grinned big enough to crack the edges of his black eyeballs. He turned and got down in front of a gray safe, back of his desk, and twisted the dial on its door. When it opened, he took out a stack of bills, closed it up and spun the dial again. Then he handed me the cash. Just like that. "Two grand it is," he said.

I took the stack and riffled through it. All hundreds. Riffled it again under my nose, for a snort of green. Then I shoved it into the pocket of my jeans. "What're the terms?"

"No worries, Jack Langer. Get yourself settled. Get a good night's sleep. Hey, I got a 'mano on auto row, you want me to hook you up?" He jerked his head toward the back door. I needed a car to look for work, so I followed him out.

A two-door, silver Caddy was parked behind the shop. Shiny, pure car porn.

"Get in," said Marco as he popped the door locks. "Let's get you set up right, vato."

I slid into a black leather seat. The beat of Latino rap erupted all around. Marco punched it. Yellow signals from a half-dozen cross streets disappeared, and we ramped up onto I-5, headed south. The smell of musky leather, the pounding reverb, two grand in my pocket and the sweet taste of freedom swallowed me whole. It felt almost like the old life sucking me in. But this time, things would be different.

Marco took us down 82nd Avenue in Southeast. Pulled into a place called EZ Way Auto. It had maybe 50 cars on the lot, all used, all bright polished metal, shimmering in the hot sun. Before we were five steps out of the Caddy, a skinny dude in a black T-shirt, hair pulled back in a ponytail, burst out of a little shack, smack in the middle of the jammed lot.

"Luis, que onda buey?" Marco said with open arms. The two of them clasped hands, and Marco bumped his shoulder into the ponytail's chest.

"This here's Jack. He's a homie from my vato, Eddie. Fresh grad out of Salem Pen."

"Luis Mendoza," the ponytail said as he offered me his boney hand. "Welcome back to the lean streets, bro. How long you in?"

"Jusy shy of two bits, but it felt longer."

"I hear that. Every day inside counts for two out here." He turned back to Marco, "So what can I do for you bros?"

"Need a deal on a carrucha for my man Jack here. What can you do for a couple of G's?"

The ponytail showed me a red Cobra pushing 200K and a Charger with most of its original paint between the dings. I settled on a '99 silver Cutlass with a V6 for $1800. It drove a little soft but it was a sweet-ass deal that left me a little slack for gas and whatnot. I hoped to hell it whatn't jacked off the street earlier that day.

Once the deal was done, I followed Marco back to his shop in St. Johns. It was after four when we rolled up behind Rapid Pawn.

"Mucho gracias for staking me, Marco."

"De nada, 'mano. It's just business."

"I'd buy you a Cuervo, but I gotta pick up my ma at work. I'll take her car. Okay to leave the Cutlass here?"

"Sure, but where do you live?"

"I'm staying with her—Tamarack Village in Scappoose."

"Hell, that's less than twenty minutes from here, right? I'll have Omar park the Cutlass up there while you pick up Mama. How do we get there?"

When I first laid eyes on him, Marco struck me as a hard case, like Eddie. But this dude was cool. I gave him the route.

"Where does your madre work?" he said as we walked up front to Ma's Maxima.

"She's the bookkeeper at Devlin's, the lumber yard in St. Helens."

"Perfecto," he said. "Al rato, vato."

I got into the Maxima and split. I could see Marco looking after me in the rearview. Thanks to him, the road back to the land of the free was looking pretty sweet. I still owed the guy two Gs, but he seemed cool with it. For once, there was nothing to worry about.

Ma was waiting outside Devlin's when I got there. She sprung for steaks at Klondike's, one of her favs, to celebrate my release. I let her drive us back to Taramack.

It was great to see the old place again, a white singlewide with light blue trim, set a little cockeyed to the curb. Dark blue steps led up to the porch, decked out with two wicker chairs, spray painted white A clump of baskets hung around the edges, spilling over with red and white flowers. The mini front yard was all white gravel, with a few large rocks painted in bright pink and blue, with a couple of potted plants thrown in to balance everything real nice, so it looked about perfect.

The Cutlass was parked on the covered pad, just like Marco promised.

"Whose car do you suppose that is?" Ma asked as she pulled up in front.

"It's mine. Picked it up in Portland, while you were at work."

"What? How did you pay for it?"

We got out of the Maxima. She locked her hands on her hips, already steaming while I checked out the Cutlass. It was locked. "A friend of a friend staked me on it." I cupped my hands against the window checking to see if the keys were inside. Nothing. "I wonder where he left the keys."

"Jack," she nabbed my arm as I checked the mailbox at the curb. "Who gave you the money? What did you have to do for it?"

Just mail in the box. I handed it over to Ma as we headed up the steps. "No worries. It's just a loan. No pressure."

From the look on her face, I could tell our little chat wasn't over. When she opened the screen, the front door creaked open. "Oh my Lord!" she said. "I'm sure I locked the door this morning!"

She cautiously led the way inside. "It doesn't look like anything's missing," she said. We both spotted the keys on the corner

I could tell our little chat wasn't over.

desk about the same time.

"Leatherface must've let himself in to drop off the keys," I explained. I cut in front of her to get them. Next to the keys was a cheap cell phone and charger. A post-it note read: WILL BE IN TOUCH. As I shoved everything into my pockets, I noticed several desk drawers were ajar. When I turned back toward Ma, her face was flushed, lips curled, ready to go off.

"Unbelievable!" She thrust her hands into the air. "This is a record even for you. In hock for a car and some lowlife breaks into my home— all in a few hours! What if I'd been here when he broke in?" She turned, as if ready to slam the front door shut. Instead, she checked herself and left it open. "I don't know why I keep thinking you're going to change." She glared at me, gesturing wildly. "I guess Bob and Steve and everybody else was right about you. You're hopeless. Forget what I said before. Forget the 30-day free ride." She clamped her arms across her chest. "I want you out. Now!"

It was like she was talking to my old man, Cy.

"Look, Ma, it's no big deal. I needed a car so I could start looking for work, right? The only reason they came in was to drop off the keys. If you'd been here, they would've handed them to you. I thought if I got a job like you wanted; if I got on it right away to show you I've changed, you'd be happy for Christ's sake."

She clenched her arms tighter against herself and glared at me. "No more, Jack. I can't take any more of your excuses."

"Just like that, eh? Thanks, Ma. Thanks for everything. Tell your friend Bob he's done a great job of turning you into a bitch."

I didn't wait for a reaction. "I'm getting my stuff; then I'm outta here."

I cut through the kitchen and went into my old room, ready to blow. Everything looked pretty much the way I remembered, but straightened away. My old bed, perfectly made up. My old posters of Half Life and The Matrix framed against freshly painted walls.

I grabbed my backpack from the closet and stuffed a few shirts and jeans inside. Threw open a dresser drawer and dug my hand under the socks and shorts until I found it. My hunting knife. Shoved everything into the pack and stomped out.

Ma was huddled in the middle of the living room couch, hand over her mouth, sort of gasping. Tracks of tears glinted off her cheeks. I stopped for a sec, but she didn't look up. She was off someplace else, some other reality. Well, me too. I slammed the door behind me.

Spent the rest of what I had at the Wig Wam that night. Hooked up with a cute little brunette for a time. But she moved on as soon the money ran out. Probably a skeeze in daylight anyway. Ended up sleeping in the back of the Cutlass, in the Wam parking lot.

As I settled in, looking up at the stars through the back window, I thought about Ma. I shouldn't have called her a bitch. She'd paid her dues long ago with the old man and deserved better.

Good 'ol Cy. What a piece of work. Always on a binge. Even at breakfast, sometimes washing down a handful of dry cereal with Jim Beam. By nighttime he'd be totally pissed. And pissed off, too. Then he'd start in on Ma. She'd just take it. As a kid, I had no idea what to do, so I'd take off. Go hide someplace. When it was warm, I'd crawl under the trailer. It muffled whatever went on inside, over my head. I kept an old blanket there to stay the night, coiled up tight like a ball of rubber bands, till I fell asleep.

In the winter, it was too cold and wet to hide there, so I'd end up at the neighbor's—Steve and Mary Temkin. In a way it was thanks to Mary we finally got rid of Cy. Steve got it into his head that my old man was boning her. Said he'd kill the bastard if his face ever showed up at Tamarack again. Any wise fool knew he'd do it, too. So Cy grabbed every cent in the house, everything worth taking, jumped in his pickup and beat cheeks. Never heard a word more.

I remember being surprised about how good it felt the second he was gone. 'Course with Ma, it was different. She teared up and had a big sob over it. I always figured she was more hurt than sad. No doubt he would've been happy to bone Mary, if she was dumb enough to let him. Even Ma got over him in a week or two.

Thinking about him always pissed me off. I needed to chill. So I started thinking about Eddie in his bunk in Salem. Wondered if he had a new cellmate yet or if he had the place all to himself for the night. Thought about Walt Hutchinson, too. Alone in the woods. Wondered how much he had stashed there. And wondered if I should reconsider the situation.

I woke to a blaring cell phone. "Hey vato." It was Marco, duh.

"Listen, something's come up. I need you to make good on that loan."

"Jesus, what're you talking about?" I ran a hand over my face. The headliner above me looked fuzzy and ragged. "When? You know I don't have any cash yet." I sat up, and the clog in my brain shifted into a new spot.

"Not my problem. I need the money back now. The rate is 50 percent, so you owe me three grand. You got till tonight to make it right. And don't be late."

"You gotta be shittin' me!" I was straight up now, kneading the front seat in my free hand. "You only gave me the cash yesterday, for Christ's sake. You gotta give me more time than that."

"I told you, it's not my problem. Three grand by 5 o'clock tonight."

"Marco, I don't have the money." Come on, man, work with me."

"You think we're having a negotiation? Me vale madre! The negotiation ended when you took my money. These are the fucking terms, you little prick. You got seven hours to make it right.

"And your mother, Eleanor Langer? Nice looking woman, just like the picture Omar found in her desk. Drives a white Maxima. Works at Devlin's in Scappoose. Gets off at five. She doesn't want you to be late with my money either."

He hung up.

Fuck! I snapped the phone shut and let it drop onto the seat. I banged my head into the back of the driver's seat and spit out curses at the bastard, at Eddie, and my sorry ass luck. But it didn't help.

I sank down in the back seat, holding my head to keep it from exploding.

No way I could go to Ma with this. Not after last night. She never had that kind of cash anyway. I picked the phone off the seat and checked the time. Six hours, 45 minutes till 5:00.

I needed a drink or a J, or something. Rolled myself over the seat to get up front. Pried open my backpack, desperate for ideas, but there was nothing but clothes. Except for the knife.

I sprung it from the sheath and tested the edge of the blade against my thumb. Sharp as shit. It felt good in my hand. Like something real. A solid, six-inch shank of steel that ran all the way through its black synthetic handle. It was a sweet blade. Except when it reminded me of my old man. Thank God, it was the only thing left of him.

I checked the cell again. Couldn't help it. It was 10:25 a.m. I needed a serious payday fast, and there was only one place I could think to get it.

I looked into the rearview mirror at my foul reflection, searching for something in my face. What choice did I have? Sometimes there isn't one. Sometimes you just have to let the universe have its way.

I pulled out of the lot and headed north on the Scappoose Vernonia Highway until Siercks Road, following the directions Eddie had etched into my brain. The scenery changed from rural homesteads to open fields. The temperature was rising.

The AC in the Cutlass was history, so I cranked the windows down and sped up to 45. The last paved mile was Pisgah Lane. The turn-off, a dirt road, just after C. C. Condon's mailbox. The name painted on the side in tall white letters, just like Eddie promised.

Rain and wear had gouged ruts into the dirt, dried and hardened by the sun. It was a struggle to steer against their pull, so I let the Cutlass slip into the tracks. The rough ride and spongy suspension on the car slowed me to a crawl. Plenty of time to check my back in the rearview. All clear across the fields behind. No witnesses. Not a sound 'cept the hiss of bugs flitting in and out of sight whenever the sun lit up their wings. You could smell the humidity. Sweet like wet grass.

As the Cutlass grumbled along, scrub trees tried for a foothold against the weeds. Maybe they'd survive another year, exposed to summer's worst. Maybe not.

It was already a scorcher, 80 degrees before noon. I swiped at the sweat trickling down my neck. It was slow going, but as long as I kept moving, the dirt and dust I stirred up, stayed behind. I thought about my next move.

I'd met several bad ass mother fuckers in the Pen. But there was one guy in particular. Dude named Thorn. I only saw him twice. They kept him in the hole full time after it happened. He got hold of a shank out in the yard. That's where he took this guy out. Shoved the blade into his neck, right under the chin and pulled it straight out the side with both hands. Must've split at least two arteries. Both of them were soaked in blood. He did it right in front of me. I had to grab onto the fence to keep my feet.

It happened so fast the guy didn't even scream. Just clung onto Thorn for a second, gurgling and foaming, eyes bugged out. Then crumpled in a heap. By the time he was on the ground, the spurting blood petered out to a steady flow. The hacks tried to save him, but there was no fucking way. He didn't last even a minute. I'll never forget it.

That's how I'll do Hutchison.

The scrub trees were getting bigger now. In the distance, closer together, they formed the edge of a woods. I heard a dog barking. The next stretch of road straightened out some, and I could see the mutt standing in one of the ruts. Black, with gray around its muzzle, snarling and barking, sounding the alarm of my approach.

"Shut the hell up," I hissed and shoved the gas pedal against the floor. My lips curled back over my teeth as the car jerked forward, pressing me into the seat. The old dog shifted over to the side of the road, half hidden in the brush, barking louder than ever. As I closed in on the fucker, I jammed the car's tires against the sides of the ruts till the car bucked clear.

Suddenly free of the pull, I oversteered and drove straight into a massive clump of thistles, shooting a swarm of goddamn bees into the air. The engine choked and stalled out. The dead stop threw me against the steering wheel. The horn blared. My head caught the edge of the rearview mirror.

I pushed myself back against the seat and slammed the heels of hands against the wheel. What miserable fucking luck. I buzzed a lungful of air through my lips and ran a hand over my forehead to check for blood. It was sopped, but only with sweat. I rubbed my hand over the sore spot where my chest had banged into the wheel; leaned over to straighten the mirror and scope out the goose egg rising on my hairline.

The dog was still barking nonstop, taunting me. I reached over to the glove box, pulled out my knife and kicked the door of the car open. The dog twitched, snarling and snapping as I closed the gap between us. I shifted my grip on the knife from the handle to the blade, ready to throw.

As I closed in, the dog started to give ground, backing all the way off the road. No matter, it would be an easy throw. I raised the knife and threw as hard as I could, slicing through the distance.

It was a perfect throw; nobody could've guessed a dog that old could move that fast, ducking to one side as my blade shot past and buried itself in the brush instead of the animal's head.

I hurled myself foward. Somehow the bastard must've sensed I was done screwing around. It turned tail and disappeared into the brush.

"Son of a bitch." I kicked the bushes where the dog had stood. Pulled the edge of my shirt up to my face, mopping my face to get the sweat out of my eyes. I ran my foot over the area where the knife should've been, but came up empty. Looked farther out and closer in, but there was no goddamn trace. Had to be somewhere, but I'd be go to hell if I could come up with it.

I hated to go on without my blade, but hated to waste any more time crawling around in the weeds too. I'd figure out how to deal with Hutchison when the time came.

I went back to the car and tried to start it. The ignition whined and grated but wouldn't catch. I pumped the gas a few times and waited while I cursed Marco for hooking me up with such a piece of

The dog twitched, snarling and snapping as I closed the gap between us.

crap. Twisted the key again and let it grind till my teeth were grinding along with the ignition. Finally it lit. I rev'ed it, shoved it into drive and coaxed it back onto the dirt road.

My shirt was pitted out by the time I coasted into the shade. Must've been ten or fifteen degrees cooler, but it barely registered. The soreness in my chest had quit and the knot on my head only hurt when I touched it. Up ahead, my first glimpse of the cabin appeared through the trees. A plain, wooden box surrounded by columns of thick tree trunks and a few leggy saplings. I stopped and cut the engine, hoping I could still take Hutchison by surprise. I got out and pushed through the brush that covered the ground, heading straight for the cabin, low and slow, like a cat on the hunt.

The sides of the cabin were covered in rough, gray planks. The roof smothered in a matt of black moss. A homemade sign that read FRESH EGGS $1.50 Dz. sat in the front window. The wooden door, set above two concrete blocks, finished off the face of Hutchison's little firetrap.

A rusty pickup was parked out front, tailgate down. A couple of chicken wire cages sat in the bed, along with a square-point shovel and a rake. Nothing I could use.

I stopped for a breath alongside the truck to listen. No breeze, no rustling of branches. The only sound came from behind the shack, the scratching and clucking of chickens. If there was a woodpile back there, maybe there'd be a hatchet.

I passed by the side of the cabin, looking up at the windows. Dark inside, with no sign of life. There was a stack of firewood out back, but whatever the guy used to split

it with was nowhere in sight.

The chicken coop was tacked onto back of the cabin, and as soon as the little cluckers caught sight of me they started squawking. Then Hutchison appeared, leaning over the back step. "What the hell are you doing out here?" he asked.

The SOB was bigger than I expected. Tall, with big hands and broad shoulders, but thin, almost gaunt. His face was pasty, a web of bluish red veins covered his nose and cheeks, disappearing under a scraggly gray beard. He was bald on top, with gray hair that spilled over the collar of a faded flannel shirt.

"You Hutchison?" I said.

"I'll ask you one more time. What the hell are you doing in my backyard?"

"Name's Jack Langer. Got a message for Walt Hutchison. That you?"

He stared at me blank faced, like he was trying to pull up a memory. When it finally came loose, he pointed a finger and said "You're Eleanor's boy, aren't you? What are doing here?"

I wondered how he knew about me, but more important, I needed to get him inside, out of sight. "You got anything to drink in there? Must be over 90° today." I wiped a handful of sweat off my face to drive the point home.

"Not much better inside, but come on. At least it's out of the sun."

He stepped back into the doorway as I climbed up the stoop. The stink on his breath, when you got near him, was unbelievable. Not like some old dude's BO, this was more like something died. Rotten, with a sort of twisted, sweet gag on it.

I turned away from him for a fresh breath, and to size up the inside. It was all one big room. Wood stove on the right. You'd think it would've dried the place out when it was stoked, but the air inside felt heavy and moist. The smell was stale, like mildew and mold. Like the man living there just didn't care.

Books were stacked every which way on blocks and boards along every wall. No TV, no computer, no phone in sight.

The bathroom was open to the room, just like a prison cell. Chevron white fixtures with reddish-brown stains, with a matching, free-standing tub. Perfect to bleed out his sorry ass in, if I'd still had my knife.

Hutchison left the door open and crossed into a sitting area as I looked around for something useful. In the kitchen area grimy dishes and empties were piled on a metal utility sink and a table next to it. Then, something caught my eye through the clutter. A boning knife.

Up to that moment it was all bluff and bull. Maybe yes, maybe no. But suddenly everything was right there. No way around it. If I was gonna to do this thing, the time had come. The world disappeared into my head. Sound slipped away. I watched as my fingers wrapped themselves around the handle of the knife. The center of my vision was sharp, but the sides faded away in a blur. I stared at the sharp edge of the knife blade. I could feel its weight in my hand. My jaw clamped tight, aching under the pressure. I remembered exactly the way Thorn did it. I turned, ready to thrust the blade into Hutchison's neck.

But the old man was ready, like he knew what was coming before I did. "What in the name of hell is wrong with you?" He was stand-ing across the room, with six or seven feet between us, his arm out straight, with a Saturday night special pointed at my heart.

"Drop it," he said.

I tossed the knife toward the sink. It clattered into the dishes.

"Sit down on the floor."

I did as he said.

Hutchison eased himself against the back of an overstuffed chair and brought his arm back into his body, gun still aimed at my chest. He had me helpless, but looked exhausted from the effort. "What's this all about?"

"Money. Nothing personal, mister. I just came here for the money. Figured I'd have to force it out of you."

"What money? Jesus Christ, have you looked around at all? What the hell made you think there's any money here?" He shifted his weight from one foot to the other and flicked the end of the gun at the room. He looked twitchy, and tired.

A new trickle of sweat ran down my face. Maybe that's what made me shiver. "My cellmate in Salem—guy named Eddie Walker—told me about you. Said you got a monthly check coming in and had a nice stash saved up here someplace. I'm into a shark big time, so I came here because I couldn't think of any easier way to score some cash."

Hutchison grimaced, sucked in a breath and pushed the air out through his mouth. That sweet, foul smell came out again, set-tling on the floor. "Eddie, fucking, Walker," he said with a smirk. "That sick bastard set us both up. Never would've thought he was smart enough to come at me from inside prison. Jesus, I guess he'll never give up till one of us is dead."

What did I get myself into?

"I sell eggs to my neighbors. Including your mother, boy. She's told me all about you. You're like, what? Twenty-two, twenty-three, and already a three-time loser?"

Too far. There was no way I could reach the old man before he'd smoke me.

"Your mother has hopes you're gonna turn yourself around, but it looks like she got it wrong. You haven't changed. You're a class-A fuck-up. Too stupid to realize you're already circling the drain. It's only a matter of time before it sucks you in."

I tried to think of a comeback, how to put a spin on it he might buy, but suddenly a Latino rap ringtune erupted into the room. I almost pissed myself. Hutchison jumped, too. "It's my cell," I said.

"Give it to me," Hutchison said as he straightened up and held out his free hand.

I slowly got up off the floor to work my hand into my jeans. Pulled out the cell and forked it over. Hutchison was distracted enough so he didn't think to order me back on my ass.

He flipped open the phone. "Hello?" He listened for a tick and then said, "Jack can't talk right now. I'll give him a message."

Hutchison locked onto my eyes while he tuned in on the caller. Then he hung up. "Marco says your mother's car broke down at work, but not to worry. He'll take care of her when she gets off."

A flood of panic shot through me from my chest to my fingertips. I reached out like I expected Hutchison to hand over the cell,

closing the space between us. Then I lunged, grabbed his gun arm and twisted into his chest. The force knocked him over with me on top. His grip went slack.

I jumped to my feet. Hutchison lay there sputtering, struggling to recover. I leveled the gun at his head. "If you got any money, old man, now's the time to tell me where it is."

He gasped and wheezed, like I'd already drilled him, his head turned to the side against the back of the chair. He shifted his eyes and glared at me, "Go to hell."

From the corner of my eye, I caught the movement of something dark. The jaws of a black dog with a grey muzzle locked onto my wrist like a coil spring trap. Its teeth cut off the blood to my hand. The gun clattered to the floor. The pain was blinding, made me dizzy. The dog's weight bent me in half. I forced myself back up, but I was losing it, blacking out. I went over backward. My head smacked against something hard. Hutchison yelled. His face swam above me. Hands around a grey muzzle. In the distance, Hutchison again, hand outstretched. A flash, a loud crack, and then nothing.

A feeling of cold and wet on my forehead. My wrist, numb and throbbing all at once. Pain at the back of my head. I let my eyes slit open. Everything blurry. Somebody's face floating over me. "Don't move," it said.

"Am I shot?" I managed to hear.

"Hardly. Just lay still. I'll be right back."

I was on the floor, arm resting across my stomach, wet rag draped over my forehead. I heard a faucet running, filling a glass. Started to move, but it sent such a stinger up my arm, I quit. Things started coming back—the old man, the black dog, the gun.

Hutchison knelt down beside me. "You're damned lucky, kid. Your wrist doesn't seem to be broken." He shoved his arm behind my back and worked me up into a sitting position.

My arm hurt like a son of a bitch, but the pain roused me. My wrist was up against me in a sling, wrapped in a wad of plastic stuffed with ice. Then it hit me. "Jesus, what time is it?"

"About half past three. You weren't out long."

"Help me up, okay?"

"Take this," Hutchison said as he shoved something through my teeth and held a glass for me to drink.

I swallowed a half dozen times, suddenly realizing how thirsty I was. "What was that?"

"Pain killer. I got plenty of 'em. It'll take the edge off and keep you civil. Now, I'll help you up, but do not give me any more of your bullshit."

"I'm done causing you trouble." I felt like the wet rag that had dropped to the floor. "I just want to get outta here."

He grabbed me under the arms from behind, helped me up on my feet and walked me over to a bench alongside a heavy wooden table. The effort zapped me. I leaned back against the table's edge to stay upright. "Listen," I said. "Marco—the guy that called—he's gonna hurt my mother, unless I stop him. You gotta let me go."

Hutchison's easy chair was flipped toward me now. He walked over to it, picked the revolver up off the seat and dropped himself into the chair.

"Shit!" I closed my eyes. "Did you call the cops on me?"

"No, but there's still plenty of time."

He had me again, more helpless than ever. But what the hell did he want?

He flicked the end of the gun toward the dog. It lay, flopped on its side, drying blood puddled up from somewhere underneath. "I had to shoot old Samson here to stop him. He would've gone for your throat next."

Jesus, I'd ruined every fucking chance I had. If I survived this, I'd never, ever, let myself in for this kind of shit again. "Look, I know you got no reason to believe me, but I couldn't be more sorry for all of this." I felt a cold shiver wash over me. "You have to let me go. I'm begging you." I could barely choke it out, "Let me save my mother."

It didn't look like he even heard me.

"Eddie Walker and I were in Nam together," he said. "Everybody was scared shitless to be over there, but no one was worse than me. I freaked out the first time we came under fire. Completely lost it. Made the worst mistake of my life. Shot Eddie's best friend in the back. Killed him. Larry Egan was his name. Just a kid, like the rest of us. It was an accident. I was officially cleared. Frankly, I could never remember what happened, but they said Larry had stepped into the line of fire. Didn't matter. I never forgave myself, and neither did Eddie."

It was hard to focus on what he was saying. Panic was rising inside me. I couldn't waste any more time. "Please, I'll do anything you want. Just let me go. For God's sake, can't you see, somehow I've gotta save Ma!"

The handgun was still pointed at me, but I could tell the old man was thinking. As we stared across the space between us, it came to me that his next move would fall out of what I'd done. And it wouldn't be good.

The corner of his mouth curled up. He opened the back of the revolver and dropped out four of the last five bullets, counting them off as they fell into his lap. Then he closed the cylinder and spun it. "Killing somebody is probably the worst thing you could ever do," he said. "Once it's done, the rest of your life is done too."

A shot of adrenaline surged through me like a shockwave. But I was frozen stiff, paralyzed.

Hutchison looked at the back of the gun as if checking which chamber the last bullet was in. He spun the cylinder again. A wicked smile spread over his face. Then raised his arm and pointed the gun at my chest. "Imagine what the victim must feel like." Then he pulled the trigger.

My heart almost burst as I heard the click of that empty chamber. I gasped out some kind of noise and clutched at the edge of the table to stop shaking.

Hutchison sank into the back of his chair, resting the gun on the worn out fabric. He choked out a deep breath. "We're almost done here," he said. "There's just one thing left for you to do."

A few days later I woke up to the weekend across from Ma's trailer. Another night cramped out in the back seat of the Cut-

He raised his arm and pointed the gun at my chest.

lass. I saved every cent of the cash that was left, refusing to spend it on food or a cheap hotel.

I was starved and decided it was time to square things. It was early, but there were signs of life in her kitchen window. I hauled myself out of the car, stretched and looked around the park. Not much action, just a few empties from last night's clubbing, and a couple of newspapers wrapped in plastic bags, waiting to be picked off the gravel and grass by the park's white collar wannabes.

I dumped the sling yesterday. My wrist was healing up good, so I was off the PKs. Still looked kinda messed up though, so I kept it hid under a long-sleeve tee. Thank God, I caught up with that fucktard Marco just in time. Walt Hutchison finally coughed up his stash. Almost four Gs. Gave me every cent he had.

I paused on the stoop, then knocked.

Ma saw me through the window and opened the door. She looked surprised, but tired. "Good morning, Jack. I hope you're here to make amends."

"Yeah, sorry about what I said before, about everything. I didn't mean any of it. I kinda been taming the beast the last couple days. I think you'd be pleased; maybe half way, anyway. I was hoping to bum some breakfast off ya . . ."

She gave me a half smile. "You want some eggs?"

"Yeah, eggs would be just the thing," I said as I followed her back to the kitchen. "Over easy, with toast." I poured a cup of joe and took my place at the table, while Ma did her thing.

"Sad news this morning," she said as she slid a pat of but-ter into a frying pan. "Did you know Walter Hutchison?"

I almost choked on the coffee. Set the mug down to cover what I'd spilled and wiped my hand off on my jeans. Took a breath to settle my nerves, to remind myself nobody knew nothing. Ma's back was to me, she didn't see a thing. "Who's that?"

"I guess you wouldn't have known him. I used to buy eggs from him from time to time. He had a little cabin north of Scappoose. Nice man."

She loaded the toaster and cracked one egg after another into the pan. I wanted the sizzle and the smell to take me back someplace else, maybe somewhere simpler, but it didn't.

"His obituary is in today's paper. Poor man committed suicide. Shot his dog and then took his own life."

She flipped the eggs gently and placed a butter knife and a jar of blackberry jam on the table. "I suppose it's all for the best, but it's still a shock to read about it in the paper like that." She slid the eggs onto a plate, added the toast and set it in front of me. "He had cancer, stomach cancer, and by the time they found it, it was already too late."

My hunger was gone now, but I had to make a show. "He probably just wanted to get it over with, so he offed himself."

She sighed and sat down across from me with her hands folded on the table. "I suppose so. The last time I saw him, he said they only gave him a few more weeks, at most. He was taking a lot of pain medicine." She shook her head and cracked a weak smile for a sec. "It's funny, he said the only thing keeping him going was that old dog of his. Maybe that's why it's such a shock. I never would've thought he'd shoot that dog."

"Maybe he was ticked off the damn dog was gonna out last him. Maybe he figured nobody else'd want it. How well did you know this guy?"

She shot me a look over the top of her glasses. "He was a recluse, in many ways. Isolated, like he was punishing himself for something. Started selling eggs—I think it was sometime while you were in Salem—to supplement his income. I'd stop over there once a month or so."

She took her specs off and set them on the table. "I told him about your troubles with the law. He said your behavior would only get worse, that you'd never change. But he didn't know you. I told him you were better than that."

She looked like she'd lost a best friend, wrung out and weepy. She wiped the circles under her eyes with the back of her hand. "Tell me you're better than that."

I couldn't bear to see that look on her face. There was no way I would ever tell her it was me that killed Walt Hutchison. A mercy killing, no doubt about that, he wanted me to do it. But I still have to live with it.

I hope I can.

I hope when Eddie hears about it he'll figure he got what he wanted all along. And I hope what he told me about intent and murder was true.

"Look Ma, I know I lost any cred I ever had. I know Cy burned you bad, and words are just words. But I'm begging you for one last chance." I reached across the table and put my good hand on top of hers and squeezed. "You gotta know there's only one chance left for me, and you're the only one who can give it. I'm asking you to put up with me till I find a job. A straight job. Get back on my feet. I swear to God, I ain't Cy all over again. There's some of you in here, too."

Richard Krauss is a writer and cartoonist. Previous work has appeared in *Copy This!, Space and Time, Satyr, Not My Small Diary, Newave!* and *Treasury of Mini Comics Vol. 1.* He lives in Portland, Oregon with his wife and family.

Matthew Turcotte Interview
Archie Comics Digest collector
By D. Blake Werts

Matthew Turcotte is a thirty-three year old customer service specialist who works for a major retail chain in Brockville, Ontario, Canada. In addition to reading and collecting Archie comics, he keeps his writing skills polished with his blog "A Pop Culture Addict's Guide to Life." Matthew's dream is to have a full-time writing career.

Curious to learn more about the vast array of Archie Comics Digest titles, TDE contributor D. Blake Werts caught up with Matthew via email for a few questions about collecting the many digests of Archie and his Riverdale gang.

The Digest Enthusiast: Hi Matthew, thank you very much for taking time to answer a few questions with us. First off, we have to get some of the basics out of the way: when did comics and/ or comic books enter your life? Do you have favorites, and if so, have your favorites changed over time?

Matthew Turcotte: I was very

young when I first began reading comic books. I think from the moment that I learned how to read, I was already reading the comics section in the daily newspapers. I recall that Peanuts, Garfield, and Archie were among my favourites. All three of those comic strips I still enjoy today, but I would say that Archie comics are my main obsession. I was

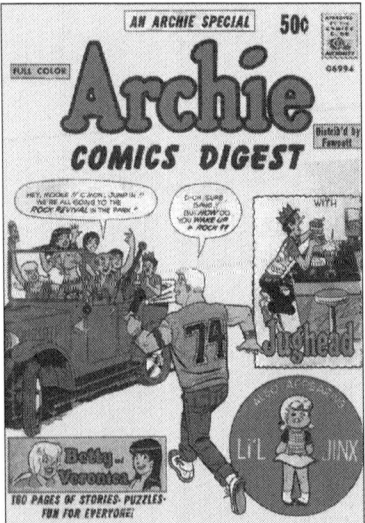

Archie Comics Digest #1 Aug. 1973

five when I received my first Archie digest, and twenty-eight years later, I have a collection in the thousands.

TDE: I was a big fan of Garfield as well. I remember a period as a kid when I was trying to learn how to draw Odie and Garfield. You were only *five* years old when you started reading Archie digests? That's quite young! And did you say "thousands?" Did you understand the mentality of "collecting" things like comic books at such an early age? Or let me ask a different way—when did you actively start methodically collecting the digest titles? And have there really been "thousands" issued to date?

MT: My Archie comic collection is well over three thousand books. Of those, I'd say that at least two thousand of those are digests and double digests. And that's not including the *Katy Keene*, *Sonic the Hedgehog*, or *Teenage Mutant Ninja Turtle* digests either! I don't know the exact number, but last time I counted, I had around 2,200

digests alone. As for whether I knew how valuable comic books were, I really had no idea as a five year old. In fact, this may seem like a stab to the heart of major comic book collectors, but I used to colour in them with permanent markers, or cut out panels I really liked and glued them in scrapbooks. I was quite the destructive five year old. Thank heavens that I live in a town with a used bookstore that sells old Archie digests so I could replace the ones I destroyed so long ago! I think by the time I was eight, I stopped my destructive ways and actively became a massive collector.

TDE: Nothing at all wrong with using your comic books as scrapbook material! I've been known to do a bit of collage work with some panels myself! Ha! 2,000+ Archie digests?! Oh man, I had no idea there were so many. We'll get in to some details a little later . . .

Since we're focusing on Archie digests and related titles, when did Archie and his many friends show up on your radar? And what about the digests in particular appealed to you?

MT: I was five years old when I read my first Archie digest, so that would be 1986–1987. My mom brought home a copy of a *Little Archie Digest* from the supermarket (one of the most common places where Archie digests are sold these days), and I just remember the cover gag as if it were yesterday. It showed Little Archie and Jughead skating on a bunch of ice cubes that Betty and Veronica were using to make an indoor skating rink. I'm not sure that would work in real life, but I found it quite entertaining! I also think that the small size of the pages (as opposed to the 32- and 48-page comics that most people grew up reading) appealed to five-year-old hands. Plus, digests were much more durable than the 32-page comics. Any 32-page comic I had as a child would have the cover torn off within five minutes, while digests tended to have more shelf life. (Of course, at 33 years old, I have since learned to take care of my comics!)

TDE: Ha! It's ironic in that I, too, purchased my first Archie digest from the local grocery. In fact, I'd say that the majority of my budding collection has come from the local grocery! Maybe you have some deep knowledge about the Archie marketing strategy so I'll ask—are you aware of Archie's approach to selling the digests via retail? Is the grocery store checkout lane a high priority for them?

MT: I have absolutely no affiliation with Archie Comics Publications directly, so your guess is as good as mine behind their marketing strategy, but I can tell you that having worked in the retail industry for almost a decade, comic books make a great impulse purchase. They certainly stand out among the other books and magazines positioned there, and they're very attractive to kids—especially in 2013–2014 when they started using neon colours on the digest covers. Twenty years ago, you'd never see neon green and orange on a cover, and now they are used almost as commonly as the standard ROY G. BIV spectrum!

TDE: Yeah, those marketing guys seem to have the market on impulse-buy positioning in the checkout lanes at the grocers here in the south. I've got to believe this practice, however much they are paying

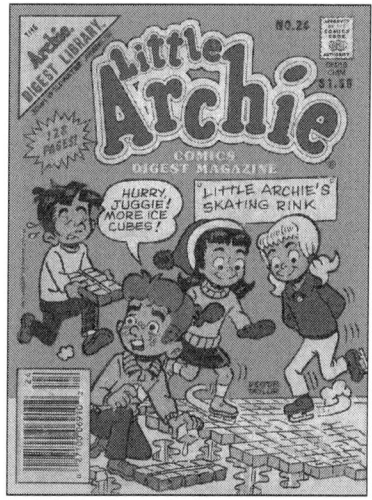

Little Archie Comics Digest #24
May 1987

to do it, is keeping them afloat.

Great story about the memory of this first digest in your collection. I have to ask you, do you still have this particular copy around in your collection? And great points about their durability. Do you still have a preference for the digests over the regular comic book today? Did you ever collect the regular Archie comic books?

MT: I do have the very first digest that I bought, though I had to replace it with another copy as the first copy had gotten a little threadbare (many of the pages were torn and had fallen out), but it definitely is one of my favourite comic books. As for collecting the standard comics, I only really started doing that recently because one nasty habit that digests do that I find annoying is trying to update stories to befit the 21st century audience. They would either change the slang around to make it seem more common (for example, changing "groovy" to "radical" to "sick"), or they'd actu-

Archie's Double Digest #145 Oct. 2003

ally redraw panels to incorporate new technology. I still laugh at one example where they tried to pass off records as CDs, even though the artist never bothered to change the size! It was like Archie and the gang were listening to laserdiscs! So, one reason why I started collecting the standard comics was to see what these stories looked like untouched and unedited.

I'd say my most prized 32-page comic thus far is *Archie's Girls Betty and Veronica* #320—Cheryl's first appearance. I got it for a great price though . . . certainly nowhere near the thousand dollars I've seen some people selling it for!

TDE: You know, I've always wondered how much of the digests were truly repeat stories from the past and how much of it was new material. My assumption is that the digests are always just collecting past work into the digest format. Has this always been the case? Is there ever any truly new material appearing in the digests? I wonder if

someone has documented all of the previous appearances of the stories, etc., in a nice reference work?

MT: It's been my experience that in the past, the first and the last stories of any random digest circa 1980–2009 are brand new stories (at the time). Usually one giveaway is the fact that they put the writer/inker/penciller credits at the beginning of the story. Of course nowadays the company does this with *every* story, so it makes it harder to tell. Usually with milestone issues (like the recent *Jughead's Double Digest* #200), they write a new story for the digest. And when they did that "New Look" experiment beginning in 2007, the first thirty pages of the digest were devoted to it.

TDE: "New Look experiment?" What was that?

MT: The New Look experiment was one that lasted approximately four years from 2007–2011. It all began in *Betty and Veronica Double Digest* #151. Artists were brought in to redraw the Archie characters in such a way that they looked like real people instead of cartoon characters. All the stories were taken from a series of Archie romance novels that were published right around the 50th anniversary. For reference sake there are seven different story arcs, each spanning four issues:

1. ***Betty & Veronica Double Digest*** #151–154 (based on *Bad News Boyfriend*)
2. ***Betty & Veronica Double Digest*** #170–173 (based on *My Father, The Enemy*)
3. ***Betty & Veronica Double Digest*** #180–183 (based on *Betty Cooper, Baseball Star*)
4. ***Archie's Double Digest*** #200–203 (based on *One*

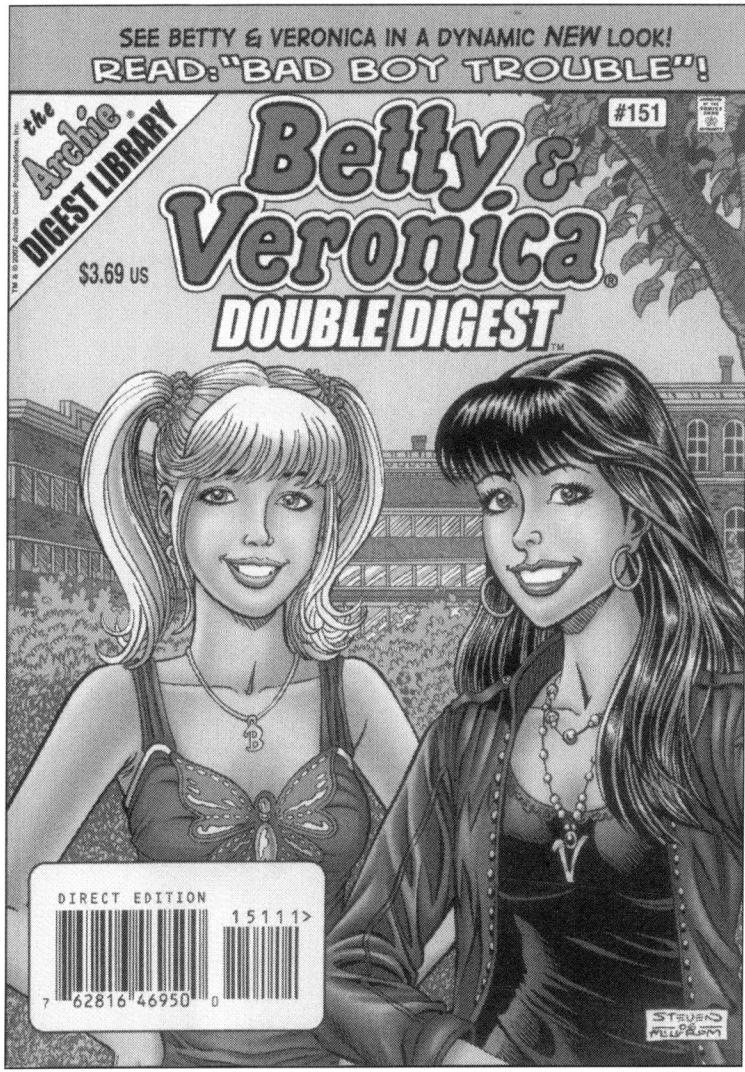

SEE BETTY & VERONICA IN A DYNAMIC *NEW* LOOK!
READ: "BAD BOY TROUBLE"!

Betty & Veronica Double Digest #151 featuring a "new look" story July 2007.

Last Date With Archie)
5. *Jughead's Double Digest* #139–142 (based on *It's First Love, Jughead Jones*)
6. *Archie's Pals N Gals Double Digest* #125–128 (based on *The Big Break-Up*)
7. *Archie's Pals N Gals Double Digest* #135–138 (based on *Class Clown*)

I would say that the digests started reprinting 32-page stories after approximately five to seven years after they originally appeared. After that, it's reprinted about every four years or so. So some of the newer stories may only be reprinted once. But I have seen stories reprinted about ten times or more. Once they even reprinted the

Betty & Veronica Double Digest #152
Aug. 2007.

Betty & Veronica Double Digest #153
Sept. 2007.

same story in consecutive issues! But that's not nearly as bad as reprinting the same exact *cover* in back to back issues. And that happened once and only once—with *B & V Friends Double Digest* #233 and #234!

TDE: That's crazy! The same cover for two consecutive issues?! Tell us a bit about your history of collecting Archie digests.

MT: From the first comic I received, I immediately fell in love with the title. Archie and the gang were like the classmates that I always wished for but never had. I was picked on a lot as a kid, and I didn't have very many friends, so I suppose the world of Riverdale acted as a sort of security blanket for me, knowing that no matter how nasty kids could be in school, I always knew one place, albeit fictional, where everyone treated everyone with kindness and respect regardless of age, gender, sexual preference, colour, or religious affiliation. I guess you could consider Archie

digests the one thing from my childhood that I refuse to let go of.

TDE: Agreed. The world of Riverdale is a fun and safe place to visit, no doubt about that. And certainly you should be able to keep Riverdale with you for as long as you'd like. Digging back into the focus of digest collecting, when did you start collecting the Archie digests as a true hobby, as something you focused on? And how has this collecting progressed over the years? Where are you in this collection now (you mentioned "thousands" earlier)?

MT: I started becoming a true collector of Archie digests when I was eight years old, so that would have been around 1989. It was shortly before Archie celebrated their 50th anniversary in 1991 which was a huge deal. I was blown away that Archie had even been around for that long, and it clicked on me that I still had five decades of stories that I hadn't read yet, so right there I made it a mission to read every single story. I started putting my comics in cardboard boxes at first and now I have one gigantic bookshelf where I store them!

TDE: So you've been actively collecting the various Archie digest titles for about 25 years now. Has this been a hobby that you've always stuck to or have there ever been periods where you've slacked off, maybe lost some interest, and came back to it later?

MT: I suppose you could say that I've been a fan of Archie for 27 years, as I started reading them in '87 approximately! And no, I never really slacked off on collecting them. Of course, when I was a kid, I missed several issues as the vast majority of my digests were bought with birthday money or tooth fairy money or weekly allowance money. When I became a teenager and had more money on my hands, I would say that my comic collecting really improved. I have not missed a consecutive digest since 2005—a personal record for me!

TDE: Now that's dedication! Let me get into a bit of your collecting process, if you don't mind. Do you subscribe to any of these titles or are you picking them up off the rack each month? How have you been adding the older releases to your collection? And how are you storing them? You mentioned a shelf earlier but I can't imagine a shelf holding 2000+ books. Are you a stickler for condition? Do you keep them in protective bags?

MT: For the most part, I do pick the books up from the rack. There is a bookstore that I frequently haunt for the recent releases. The only time I've ever subscribed to

Betty & Veronica Double Digest #170 June 2009.

a digest title is when for whatever reason the store forgets to order a certain title (I had to do this with *Jughead's Double Digest* a couple of years back). One thing I will say about the Archie people is that their subscription department is fairly reasonable. I mean, I did get the titles the same week they came out on the newsstands, but I chalk it up to the fact that I live in Canada, and shipping from the U.S.A. to Canada is a slow process at times!

Now because I was born in 1981, I was obviously too young to get the older digests. As mentioned, we have a used book store in town that sells a lot of older digests, and I have bulked up the majority of my collection from that store. But I also shop at online stores like eBay or NewKadia . . . sometimes I've even bought books from people who are a part of Archie comic forums. I can't remember what book it was, but one of my digests was purchased from Australia. The

Jughead's Double Digest #53 Aug. 1998.

shipping cost an arm and a leg, but it must have been worth it. Now that I think of it, it could have been *Archie Digest* #1. I can't remember though. Still, my collection literally comes from all over the globe!

I don't have my digests sealed in bags. Unlike some hard core comic collectors, I like to read and re-read my comics every once in a while. My 32-page comics are mostly bagged though. And my shelf right now is three deep, which means that I can put three stacks of books on the same shelf. Makes it impossible to read the ones in the very back, but it's economical enough for it to do— just at least until I get more space.

TDE: Don't hesitate to name/recognize your bookshops by name if you'd like. Let us all support those remaining shops that do still exist!

MT: The name of the used book store I frequent is called Book Trader located in Brockville, Ontario, Canada. When I first started shopping there though, it was known as Mulberry Hill Books. They do sell

other comic book collections too. At one point, they had nearly the entire Garfield and Far Side collections.

TDE: So you're not cherry-picking minty-fresh copies when you are out shopping for new additions to the collection? What about the older issues you are buying to fill holes? What is your desired condition requirements? Or does it even matter to you?

MT: Yes, I still have a tendency to try and replace old worn out copies of books. I'm not too fussy on mint condition books, but I would like them to stay in at least a Fine condition. I've been doing quite well with preserving the ones I do have though!

TDE: I'm curious, when you subscribed to an Archie digest, how did they come in the mail? Were they protected in any way or did they simply stick an address label on the digest cover (the horror!)?

MT: I don't know how it was back in the olden days, but when I subscribed to any comics from Archie Comics, the books were always in plastic bags, and the address label was stuck on the bag itself. I could only imagine the outcry that would have happened had the labels been stuck to the actual book themselves!

TDE: Believe me, today some of the other digest magazines like *Analog* and *Ellery Queen*, you have to pay extra to get them shipped in plastic baggies; otherwise they are shipped "naked" with a nasty paper address label stuck right on the front cover! Nasty!

Speaking of filling holes in the collection. How far away are you from having all that have been released? Have you completed any specific titles thus far?

MT: I think it might be easier to list the titles that *I don't* have completed! I have mostly complete sets. And the ones I don't (*Archie Digest, Archie's Double Digest, Jughead With Archie Digest, Laugh Digest*), I'm only missing three or four at the most. I would say I'm around 15–25 books that I still need to have a complete digest collection.

TDE: Now that's quite an accomplishment! Are there some titles/issues that you have found to be harder to locate? Any collecting tips that you can share with our readers?

MT: I don't really have any collecting tips, other than checking online stores and auction sites every day. You never know what you'll find. Also, hit up garage sales, Goodwill shops, or flea markets. It's rare, but you could probably find comics there as well. And, I suppose if you had extra money, you could pick some books up at comic book conventions, though I can't say for sure, as I've never attended one.

As for titles, I haven't had much trouble finding specific titles, though finding #1 issues was a real pain for me. I'm still missing the first issue of *Jokebook Digest*. And there was one instance in which I was missing one issue from having a complete set (I believe it was *Jughead Jones Digest*). It took me eighteen *years* to complete it!

TDE: What?! Likely the cat with the largest Archie comics collection and you've never been to a comic book convention?

MT: I know, it sounds really odd that I haven't been to a convention, but there's a good reason for it. Most of the really good ones (San Diego, NYC) are too far away and they would be a

Jughead Jones Digest #76 July 1992.

little on the pricey side. That said, I would love to attend at least one!

TDE: Very likely the majority of our readers will not be "hip" to the Archie digest titles. Can you help educate us on the various digest titles and name changes that have happened over time? When did Archie Comics start appearing in digest format?

MT: The very first Archie digest title was obviously *Archie Digest* #1. And believe it or not, it was released in the summer of 1973—making the *Archie Digest* 41 years old!

As of 2014, there are seven different digest titles. Below, I'll list the titles that exist now, and what they used to be called (none of the current digest titles are originals, sadly).

1. ***Archie Comics Digest*** (previously *Archie's Double Digest*)
2. ***Betty and Veronica Comics Digest*** (previously *Betty and Veronica Double Digest*)

Now here's where it gets really confusing.

3. **World of Archie Comics Digest** (previously *World of Archie Double Digest*, which was previously *Archie Digest*)

4. **B & V Friends Comics Digest** (previously *B & V Friends Double Digest*, which was previously *Betty & Veronica Digest*)

5. **Archie's Funhouse Comics Digest** (previously *Archie & Friends Double Digest*, which was previously *Archie's Pals N Gals Double Digest*)

6. **Jughead and Archie Comics Digest** (previously *Jughead's Double Digest*)

7. **Sonic Super Digest**

Listing all the titles published by the Archie Digest Library:

1. **Archie Digest**
Aug. 1973–Nov. 2010
(267 issues)

2. **Jughead with Archie Digest**
Mar. 1974–May 2005
(200 issues)

3. **Laugh Digest** Aug. 1974–Apr. 2005 (200 issues)

4. **Archie Annual Digest**
Summer 1975–Apr. 1998
(Spans from #27-69)

5. **Mad House Digest**
1975–1982 (8 issues)

6. **Archie...Archie Andrews... Where Are You? Digest**
Feb. 1977–May 1998
(114 issues)

7. **Jughead Jones Digest**
June 1977–May 1996
(100 issues)

8. **Little Archie Digest**
1977–May 1991 (48 issues)

9. **Jokebook Digest**
1977–1983 (13 issues)

10. **Archie's Super Hero Digest**
1978–1979 (2 issues)

11. **Betty and Veronica Digest**
1980–Dec. 2010 (208 Issues)

12. **Pat the Brat Digest**
1980 (1 issue)

13. **Captain Hero Digest**
1981 (1 issue)

14. **Archie's Double Digest**
(now *Comics Digest*)
Jan. 1982–current
(current issue #254)

15. **Archie's Activity Digest**
July 1985–Aug. 1986 (4 issues)

16. **Archie's Story & Game Digest**
Nov. 1986–Jan. 1998
(39 issues)

17. **Betty & Veronica Double Digest** (now *Comics Digest*)
June 1987–current
(current issue #226)

18. **Katy Keene Digset**
Mar. 1988–July 1990
(10 issues)

19. **The New Archies Digest**
May 1988–July
1991 (14 issues)

20. **Betty & Veronica Annual Digest** 1989–Aug. 1997
(16 issues)

21. **Jughead's Double Digest**
Oct. 1989–Apr. 2014
(200 issues)

22. **The New Little Archie Digest**
July 1991–Mar. 1998
(21 issues)

23. **Veronica's (Passpost) Digest**
Nov. 1992–Oct. 1997 (6 issues)

24. **Archie's Pals N Gals Double Digest** Nov. 1992–Jan. 2011
(146 issues)

25. **Teenage Mutant Ninja Turtles Classics Digest**
Aug. 1993–Dec. 1994
(7 issues)

26. **Archie: All Canadian Digest**
Aug. 1996 (1 issue)

27. **Betty's Digest** Nov. 1996–
Nov. 1997 (2 issues)

28. *Archie's Holiday Fun Digest*
Feb. 1997–Dec. 2007
(12 issues)

29. *Tales from Riverdale Digest*
June 2005–Oct. 2010
(39 issues)

30. *Jughead and Friends Digest*
June 2005–Aug. 2010
(38 issues)

31. *World of Archie Double Digest* (now *Comics Digest*)
Dec. 2010–current
(current issue #43)

32. *B & V Friends Double Digest* (now *Comics Digest*)
Jan. 2011–current (starts at #209, current issue #240)

33. *Archie and Friends Double Digest*
Feb. 2011–Jan. 2014 (33 issues)

34. *Sonic Super Digest*
Dec. 2012–current
(current issue #8)

35. *Archie's Funhouse Comics Digest* Feb. 2014–current
(current issue #8)

36. *Jughead & Archie Comics Digest* Jun. 2014–current
(current issue #5)

Plus the two digests for Free Comic Book Day, the six 1000-page digests, and one *Archie Giant Comics Digest.*

TDE: What are your thoughts on the retail prices of the digests today ($4.99–$6.99)? And for the older issues, from a collect-ability point of view, what are collectors expected to pay to add those issues to their collections?

MT: Well, it makes me cringe to see prices so high because when I first started reading Archie digests, they were $1.25 for a single digest, and $2.25 for a double digest! But inflation happens. And now they periodically release Jumbo digests

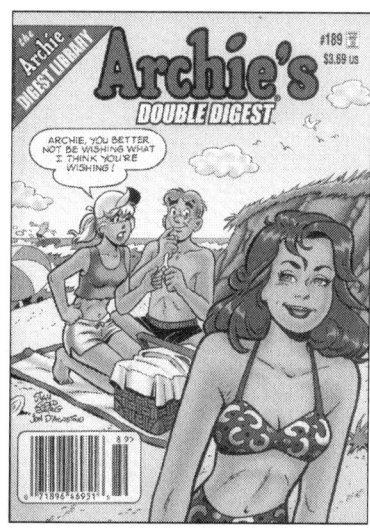

Archie's Double Digest #189 Aug. 2008.

which can be almost $10 a book— but the pro is you get twice as many pages. So, I guess I understand why prices are increasing. After all, digests seem to sell better than 32-page comics these days. As for older books, it wouldn't be unreasonable to spend more on them, especially if the condition is near mint. Of course, if you just want reading copies, you can easily get whole lots on eBay for as little as $5.00 each.

TDE: True the prices are indeed higher. Of course, you've seen the tendency for even the thin 32-page comic books to run $3.99 and more, right? Where this is headed I have no idea. I've got to believe there will be some limit and even the kids will have to stop buying because they are so damn expensive. But that's just me blowing off steam here.

Have you done any re-search work into publication/sales numbers on Archie comics and digests? I'd be curious to see where the trends are headed.

MT: I personally haven't done

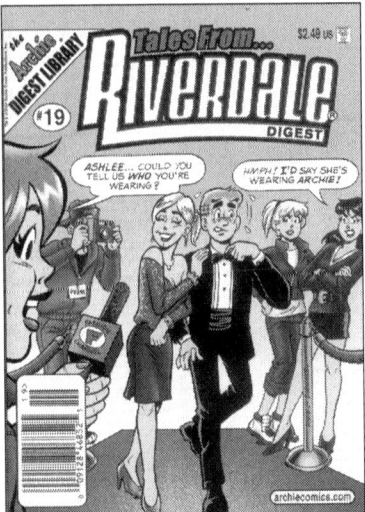

Tales from Riverdale Digest #19
May 2007.

any research on these trends yet, but I am sure several other people have. A quick Google search could probably get some statistics.

TDE: What kind of price range on the older digests have you been paying for copies in better condition? Are we talking $5 each or $10 each or $25 each? Can you give us a sense of what the retail/resale market is like on these digest back issues today?

MT: It really depends on the place you're buying the older books. The used book store I frequent charges a dollar per digest, which is quite good. But if you're buying online, expect to pay more. A lot of online comic retailers charge by the condition. If a book is graded as Good, you may pay about $2 a book, but if it's graded Near Mint, you may pay up to fifteen times that price. I would imagine that *Archie Digest* #1 would be worth more than say, *Betty and Veronica Double Digest* #193, for instance.

TDE: Any recommendations for those that are interested in starting a collection of Archie digests?

MT: Well, how I would approach collecting is to first choose a title that you enjoy, and secondly, choose a title in which you can easily find books that are relatively cheap. I would also recommend buying newer issues first before you start looking for older books. You could easily find lots of digests within the last 15 years for a really decent price.

TDE: Thanks for sharing a bit of your history and collecting of Archie Comics with us Matthew. I can say that my interest in the titles have certainly increased! As we wrap up, let me ask about your favorite Archie character(s)? Favorite story line(s)? Best memory(ies) with Archie digests? Favorite time period of the digests that you have enjoyed the most? Do you have any favorite writers and/or artists? Maybe a favorite storyline that you've enjoyed?

MT: Thank you Blake. This has been really fun.

My all-time favourite character is Jughead. I have practically every single Jughead digest printed (save for a couple of issues of *Jughead with Archie Digest*). There's just something about his non-conformist attitude that was refreshing. Most people do everything they can to fit in, but Jughead did everything he could to do anything but fit in. The refreshing part was that people liked him anyway. Kind of gave "square pegs" like myself a little bit of hope.

For favourite time periods . . . I myself am partial to the 1980s era, as that was when I started reading the comics. A lot of current artists like Dan Parent began their careers during that same decade, so I literally grew up reading their stuff my whole life. Aside from the 1980s, I also enjoy 1970s era stories, only because they tended to be a little more risqué and daring than they are now. I would say that Archie comics have seemingly been watered down a little bit since the seventies, but as for what I would attribute that to, I don't know. Maybe parent complaints?

Favourite artists for me include Dan DeCarlo, Samm Schwartz, Dan Parent, Stan Goldberg, and Harry Lucey. For recent artists, I also like Fernando Ruiz and Rex Lindsey. Really, anyone who draws Jughead is a favourite of mine. As for writers, I always seemed to like stories written by Frank Doyle or George

Gladir. Both of them seemed to understand who the Archie gang really was, if that makes sense.

TDE: If you'd like to give us a list of what issues are missing from your collection, maybe one or more of our readers can help out?

MT: A list of ones I'm missing, huh? I suppose there's no harm in that:

Archie Digest #4
Jughead with Archie Digest #6
Laugh Digest #2, 3, 11, 19, 25
Archie Annual Digest #33
Little Archie Digest #2
Jokebook Digest #1
Archie's Double Digest #2, 14

So, as you can see, I'm only a few away from a complete digest set!

Archie Digest Library Triva

Finally, here are some interesting Archie digest trivia Matthew shared:

• The *Archie Annual Digest* doesn't begin at issue #1. Remember that the *Archie Annual* title began as a Giant Series style comic book. The first issue it became a digest was #27, in 1975.

TDE: Archie comics switched to printing on recycled paper in 1992. Was it the same year that their digests went from 128 pages to 96 pages, and their double digests went from 256 pages to 192 pages?

MT: I don't know if the switch to recycled paper was the cause of that, but I found it a little bit annoying that my digests shrank while the price increased! Oh well . . . I suppose if it saved trees, it was worth it.

• As well, the current Jumbo Comics (the ones that increased to 320-page digests every couple of issues or so), are reprinting classic

material from the 1940s and 1950s, which I think is an awesome idea. It will attract new fans to the serial, but will allow older fans to reminisce about their favourite comics. As well, four digests have reprinted classic first issues in their entirety:

Archie #1 (1943) in *Archie Digest* #236.

Archie's Girls Betty & Veronica #1 (1951) in *Betty and Veronica Digest* #185.

Archie's Pal Jughead #1 (1949) in *Jughead's Double Digest* #138.

Archie's Rival Reggie #1 (1949) in *Archie's Pals N Gals Double Digest* #133.

And each digest contains a new story of the characters going down Memory Lane where they meet their 1940s counterparts. If you are a collector, definitely seek these issues out! ↙

Opening Lines

Select openings from yesterday's digests.

"She first attracted his attention in an illustrated advertisement in a men's magazine."
"Party Girl" by Joseph Commings,
The Saint Mystery Magazine, October 1965

"In all the world about him there was not one thing he recognized— not one face was familiar. He was not even certain that the organisms of the beings he saw were similar to those he should know about."
"The Track of the Beast" by Charles V. De Vet,
Other Worlds Science Stories, August 1952

"Billy Neeks had a flexible philosophy regarding property rights. He believed in the proletarian ideal of shared wealth—as long as the wealth belonged to someone else."
"Snatcher" by Dean Koontz,
Night Cry, Fall 1986

"The few times I had seen Price Carroway alive I had smiled. People just don't get that fat and still walk around. But when I saw him dead, I felt like a laughing."
"Trapped" by Milton Lesser,
Pursuit Detective Story Magazine #2, Nov. 1953

"Two little boys, swimming naked in the reservoir, found the body on September 16. They saw something floating far out in the pond and swam to it and when they drew close and saw it was a dead man, they swim back to shore, jumped into their clothes and ran down the road until they saw some men working on the telephone line."
The Man Who Murdered Himself by Geoffrey Homes, A Century Mystery novel © 1936

"Their origin was as much a mystery as ever, even though they have progressed from pony carts to Cadillacs to spaceships. Dark skinned, laughable, unscrupulous, they sped across the Galaxy and occasionally stopped to ply their ancient trades and leave amusement or annoyance in their wake."
"Caravan" by H. A. Stucke,
Universe Science Fiction, November 1954

Read a digest story opening that grabbed you? Send your favorite opening lines, along with the story title, author, digest title, date and year of publication. Send to arkay@larquepress.com or
Larque Press
6327 SW Capitol Hwy, Suite C #293, Portland, OR 97239.
We'll publish the best selections next time. Contributors with selected entries will receive a limited edition *Digest Enthusiast* trading card.

10399349R00066

Printed in Great Britain
by Amazon.co.uk, Ltd.,
Marston Gate.